39429

D1379432

© THE BAKER & TAYLOR CO.

Evita

THE OFFICIAL EDITION
THE INTERNATIONAL STAGE SUCCESS

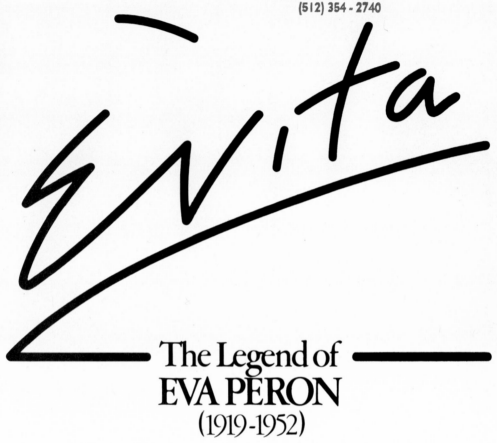

Evita

The Legend of
EVA PERÓN
(1919-1952)

by ANDREW LLOYD WEBBER *Composer*
and TIM RICE *Lyricist*

DRAMA BOOK SPECIALISTS (PUBLISHERS)
NEW YORK

AUTHOR'S NOTE (March 1978)
A work such as *Evita* constantly changes as it moves from one form to another, such as from record to stage. The bulk of *Evita* has not been altered since the release of the original double album on MCA Records in November 1976, but the discerning reader of this book will notice that several changes in the lyrics have taken place since that time. There have also been changes in the musical construction of *Evita*, but these are not obviously apparent here.

Published by arrangement with Avon Books

Library of Congress Catalog Card No. 79-53888
ISBN 0-89676-030-8

Printed in the United States of America

10 9 8 7 6 5 4 3 2 1

INTRODUCTION

Not all of the many fantastic stories told about Eva Peron are true; but any of them could be true – she was an extraordinary woman. Anyone writing about her has no need to exaggerate in order to give his work a little colour; the most straightforward account of her short life will contain enough material to raise the most sophisticated of eyebrows. That is why we chose her as the subject of an opera which we began writing in early 1974.

After the phenomenal success (in commercial terms) of *Jesus Christ Superstar* it took us some time to get to grips with a new project. *Superstar* was first released in record form in October 1970 and from that moment on became a juggernaut of a property careering around the world in every conceivable form. Judgements about the work were usually extravagant – it was either the greatest thing the world of popular music had seen or the most ghastly; of course it was neither of these.

We considered many ideas for our next effort together during the first three years of *Superstar*'s success, but partly because we were so busy trying to keep up with our hit's international progress and partly because we were a little nervous about even attempting to write a follow-up, we did nothing of any note from 1970–1973 except adapt our 1968 children's musical *Joseph and the Amazing Technicolor Dreamcoat* for a run in the West End. The work done on *Joseph* proved to be invaluable for that show went on to become one of the most-performed pieces in theatres all over Britain after its West End stint, but apart from this useful boost to our old repertoire, the only news the waiting world heard from us until 1974 was news of *Superstar*'s latest box-office success.

This may not have worried the waiting world, but it worried us. We did not want to rush into a new venture for the sake of it, but at the same time we were keen to prove that whatever abilities we possessed had not dried up. When I heard the last ten minutes of a programme about Eva Peron on my car radio one evening late in 1973, I was *not* immediately struck by the idea that here was the perfect story for us, but I was sufficiently intrigued by what I had heard to make a point of listening to a repeat of the programme a few days later. My previous knowledge of Eva Peron was negligible. I knew that she had appeared on many Argentine stamps when I was at school, that she was good-looking and she was dead. By the time I had heard the whole of the programme about her, I was hooked on the story of her life.

Not, I hasten to add, on her philosophy or her morals. It is not unreasonably assumed by most people that a composer or writer admires the heroes or heroines he writes about. This is no problem if your subject is St Francis or Florence Nightingale but one's motives can be misunderstood if the subject is a person who was indisputably murky in both character and deed. If the subject also happens to be one of the most glamorous women who ever lived, you will inevitably be accused of glamorizing her.

I cannot imagine that *Evita* will convince anybody that the tactics adopted by the Perons in the forties and fifties form an acceptable political creed, but for the record I would like to state here that the only political messages we hope emerge from the work are that extremists are dangerous and attractive ones even more so, and that a nation does not have to be a tin-pot banana republic to allow a person of the far left or far right to gain power – Argentina in 1945 was a sophisticated nation and no country today, certainly not Britain, can claim with confidence that 'it can't happen here'.

There are things to admire about Eva Peron the person – her determination to succeed against almost insuperable odds, her championing of women in a male-dominated society, her championing of her class in a class-ridden society, her courage in illness and in death, and not least her physical appearance. Even those who have written the most vitriolic accounts of her life are clearly fascinated by her, and I plead guilty to this charge too. It is a tragedy that her talents were often warped and misdirected, that her colossal energy was rarely used for more worthy ends. Even as a struggling actress in her early days in Buenos Aires, she dedicated herself to perfecting the art of manipulating people in order to become a star, rather then dedicating herself to becoming a good actress.

The case against Eva Peron is outlined throughout the bulk of this book. No one can fail to be disgusted by many of the actions of the Peronist regime, by the torture, corruption, deception, and by the gross mismanagement of a rich country. However there is a case for Eva Peron. Well aware that her credits will be heavily outweighed by the debits recounted in the lyrics and commentaries that follow this introduction, I shall say what can be said in her favour.

But first let me continue with the story of the creation of *Evita*. After Andrew Lloyd Webber and I had agreed that the story of Eva Peron could be the one strong enough to follow *Superstar*, I wrote a fairly long plot synopsis which in due course underwent many drastic changes, but even in its earliest form enabled Andrew to start work on one or two of the most important musical themes. The fact that one of these was the melody for what eventually became 'Don't Cry For Me Argentina' was very encouraging for me – it was good to know virtually from the word go that *Evita* would have at least one extremely strong tune. I still feel it is the best tune that Andrew has written to date.

I actually went to Argentina in February 1974 which was when I wrote most of the initial synopsis. I was content to maintain a low profile during my visit as both the planned stage and film presentations of *Superstar* in Buenos Aires had met with fairly strong critical reaction in that the theatre where the stage show was scheduled to open was burned to the ground and the cinema due to show the film was bombed. I am not sure exactly who was responsible but after that reaction to our work mere words from theatre critics hold no terror for me. I did not do any major research in Argentina but obviously it was a great help, and also very exciting, to see for myself many of the places where Eva Peron had operated. Buenos Aires is a magnificent city.

I think that we both felt while we were writing *Evita* that the work would eventually be finished, but it took us a long time to get it into a state fit enough to make sense to friends and colleagues. By the end of 1975 we reckoned that we had written a piece that was worth taking a stage further – there were still many improvements to be made, but if *Evita* was ever to progress beyond our interpretation of it (piano and weak vocals) now was the time. We had to decide whether to record it or whether to see if anybody would stage it.

We decided that we would launch the property via records. We had gone this route very successfully with *Superstar*, although had anybody shown the slightest interest in staging it when it was first written we would never have made the original record album. By accident we had discovered a very good way of introducing a musical work intended for the theatre – don't risk it in the theatre straightaway, test reaction to the music alone on records first. There are so many things that can go wrong with a stage musical that the writers of the score of a flop can never be really sure whether they were to blame.

We spent 1976 planning the recording, making the recording, and in November that year our work finally saw the light of day when the double record-album of *Evita* was released in Britain. During the following twelve months it proved to be very popular in many countries worldwide, with the notable exception of Argentina, where sad to say the recording has been banned.

This book does not set out to be the definitive biography of Eva Peron. In my opinion that has been written by Mary Main whose book *The Woman With The Whip* first appeared in 1952, the year of Eva's death. This excellent work was not published in Britain until 1977, a publication no doubt inspired by the success of our record. I find this ironic because I was unable to obtain a copy of the book anywhere when I was writing the lyrics of *Evita* and it would have been a great help to me.

From her earliest age, Eva Peron was consumed with a desire for power. That desire was fuelled by her bitter resentment of the fact that she was born without privileges, and that many would never

want her or accept her because of her humble origins. If she could not achieve respectability in the eyes of the established system, then that system would have to be replaced. There have been many people in many societies who have gone through their lives with similar thoughts — but few turned their thoughts into actions as Evita did.

Most people who make any kind of impact upon their fellow men owe a great deal to chance. Events and people around them have to be just right to enable their particular talent or characteristic to leap into prominence. An obvious example is Winston Churchill — in less dramatic circumstances than those of Britain in 1940 he might never have been chosen to lead his country. Had an opportunist with the efficiency of Juan Peron not crossed Eva's path in 1944, it is doubtful whether even she would have made any lasting

impression on Argentine life and politics. The combination of Peron and Eva was the factor that was the greatest single help to them both.

When Peron finally achieved power in Argentina, he produced 'justicialism' (justicialismo) as his official doctrine. Justicialism was promoted by Peron as being the alternative to both capitalism and communism, a 'third position' between that of East and that of the West. In fact Peron presided over nothing more or less than common or garden fascism, but the concept of justicialism was a perfect focus for Eva's fantasy of being a leader in pursuit of an ideal. Without her the story of Peron's presidency (assuming that he would have become president without her help) would have merely been one more depressingly typical tale of dictatorship in Latin America.

Frankly, it is impossible to say why Eva Peron reacted so drastically to the disadvantages of her

early life, when nearly every other person starting out in similar circumstances in Argentina made little attempt to alter the hand dealt out by fate. One can only say, rather obviously, that her basic make-up was different. However, once she had set out on the path she had chosen for herself, it is easy to see how no one triumph or achievement satisfied her, how ambition became megalomania, and how power became a drug that she had to pump into her system in an ever-increasing quantity. It is harder to cope with an ambition fulfilled than it is to achieve the ambition in the first place; I hope that Che's song to Eva in *Evita*, 'High Flying Adored', illustrates a little of her dilemma.

No one can blame Evita for wanting to fight her way out of the gutter; how sad that in doing so determination and viciousness became confused and remained thus even when she was the First Lady of Argentina. All the same, there was certainly a genuine desire to see an improvement in Argentine social justice caught up in the tangle of Eva's emotions right until the very end of her life; could a totally selfish person have got through the final grim months with so much dignity? She had to believe she was dying for her people, which she was able to do because she really believed she had been their saviour since 1945.

We hope that some of the life and magic, death and disaster of this strange woman is captured by the lyrics, commentaries and photographs of this book. However this work must be regarded as a companion to the recording or to the stage presentation of *Evita*, as without the music our portrait of Eva Peron is obviously incomplete.

The case for Eva Peron? She had style, in spades.

TIM RICE

1 : A Cinema in Buenos Aires, 26 July 1952

We are in a cinema in Buenos Aires on the above date. A fairly dire movie is in progress — black and white, probably of U.S. origin with Spanish voices dubbed. The film grinds to a halt. The reason is soon made clear to the audience — Eva Peron, the First Lady of Argentina, wife of President Juan Peron, has died.

'Until this moment my lips have not dared to speak of my love for you.'
'Oh Carlos!'
'And they shall do more than speak to you — my senses are flooded with desire.'
'Oh Carlos!'
'Was that a boot on your father's gravel? If it's that bounder Rodolphe, my sword will not remain long unsheathed!'
'Be careful, Carlos!'

There is an announcement from the Secretary of the Press:

It is the sad duty of the Secretary of the Press to inform the people of Argentina that Eva Peron, spiritual leader of the nation, entered immortality at 20.25 hrs. today.

We hear the above speech in Spanish. Che and the other moviegoers leave the cinema in silence.

Our version of the Eva Peron story begins with a short scene in a Buenos Aires cinema on the day she died, 26 July 1952. The film is halted by the announcement of her death. The crowd leave the cinema — all places of entertainment, shops and businesses were to remain closed for three days, and it was weeks before life in the city returned to normal.

The film soundtrack we created for the original record of *Evita* is not part of an actual movie, and its plot is totally unimportant. The idea for this opening scene came after we spoke to an Argentine friend who told us he was in a cinema when this news was announced.

2: Requiem for Evita/Oh What A Circus

Eva's funeral. Che is the only non-participant we see. After some time he moves away from the crowds.

CHE

O what a circus! O what a show
Argentina has gone to town
Over the death of an actress called Eva Peron
We've all gone crazy
Mourning all day and mourning all night
Falling over ourselves to get all of the misery right

O what an exit! That's how to go!
When they're ringing your curtain down
Demand to be buried like Eva Peron
It's quite a sunset
And good for the country in a roundabout way
We've made the front page of all the world's papers today

Although there is no evidence whatsoever that Ernesto 'Che' Guevara ever met Eva Peron or became personally involved with her, our character Che is based upon this legendary revolutionary. Guevara was an Argentinian born in 1928, who would therefore have been twenty-four years old when Eva Peron died. He became violently opposed to the Peron regime and was involved in anti-Peronist plots in the early 'fifties. In 1953 he qualified as a doctor, but left Argentina shortly afterwards. As a medical student he had at one point studied tropical diseases which led him to attempt the commercial manufacture of an insecticide in 1950.

After leaving his home country in 1953 he moved through many Latin American countries, always making contact with left-wing and/or revolutionary groups, although playing no major military role in any of the places he visited until he arrived in Mexico in summer 1955. Mexico itself was not to be a nation in whose annals the name of Guevara was to be writ large, but it was there that Che met Fidel Castro. Castro planned to invade Cuba and to release his homeland from the control of its U.S.-backed (not always enthusiastically) dictator, Batista. Castro recruited Che, although an Argentinian, to his cause as the expedition's doctor. However, a strong bond of friendship between Castro and Guevara resulted in Che's influence on the enterprise going far beyond the revolution's first-aid kit.

The invasion party (less than 100 men in one boat) reached Cuba in November 1956. The campaign got off to a disastrous start — the entire commando was nearly wiped out by Batista's air force. But neither Castro, nor Guevara, nor the cause, was destroyed and the next two years saw the remarkable growth of Castro's movement — and of the Guevara reputation. His military exploits and revolutionary zeal during this guerilla war were certainly vital factors in the overthrow of Batista by Castro at the end of 1958. The seeds of the Guevara legend had been sown. He devoted the next eight years to Cuba, but in a less comfortable (for him) semi-ambassadorial, semi-political, role — at one time being president of the National Bank of Cuba and Minister of Industry. In April 1964 he disappeared and the legend grew.

His whereabouts in 1964 and 1965 have never been satisfactorily established, but he was 'sighted' nearly everywhere. It is certain, though, that in November 1965 he arrived in Bolivia to begin what he saw as the next phase of his revolutionary contribution to history. He had ambition way beyond guerilla warfare and social change in

Bolivia, and visions of launching the whole of South America onto a totally new course. But his dreams were snuffed out in the Bolivian mountains in October 1967 where he and his army, who had never begun to repeat his Cuban successes, were trapped and killed. His early death guaranteed the immortality of his legend. This much he has in common with Eva Peron.

Che in *Evita* is at times a narrator, at times a critic, at times simply a device that enables us to place Eva in a situation where she is confronted with lucid personal criticism. His comments throughout reflect what Che Guevara might have said had he been a first-hand witness to many of the episodes of the work, but the fact that he is based on Guevara in this way is not as important as the fact that our Che represents a conventional radical opposition to Peronism.

Che's first appearance in *Evita* is at her funeral. This was a spectacular affair, to say the least — a combination of the magnificent excesses of both Hollywood and the Vatican, with huge crowds, much pageantry, wailing and lamentation. Che is the only non-participant we see. He launches into a bitter attack upon the circus of her funeral and upon Eva herself.

In the original version of *Evita*, that available on the double album released in November 1976 before any stage or film version, some of Che's anti-Eva Peron sentiments were shown to be a result of his frustrations in being unable to get anywhere with his ambitions to make money out of his insecticide, but this aspect of his anger did not appear in the opera's subsequent forms. Instead, Che's gradual disillusion with all things Peron is shown to be primarily a result of his political and idealistic disappointments.

'Evita' is simply an intimate distortion of the name Eva, and it was by this sobriquet that Eva Peron was known to those who loved her. Those who did not used other nicknames.

The Casa Rosada — the 'pink house' — is the impressive pink presidential palace that dominates the Plaza de Mayo, a great square in the centre of Buenos Aires. The Perons made many dramatic and important speeches from the balcony of the Casa Rosada.

But who is this Santa Evita?
Why all this howling hysterical sorrow?
What kind of goddess
Has lived among us?
How will we ever
Get by without her?

She had her moments — she had some style
The best show in town was the crowd
Outside the Casa Rosada crying 'Eva Peron'
But that's all gone now
As soon as the smoke from the funeral clears
We're all going to see — and how! — she did nothing for
 years!

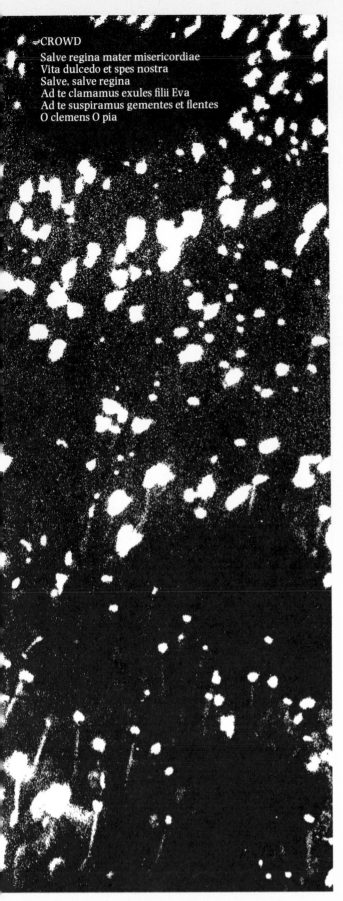

CROWD

Salve regina mater misericordiae
Vita dulcedo et spes nostra
Salve, salve regina
Ad te clamamus exules filii Eva
Ad te suspiramus gementes et flentes
O clemens O pia

This Latin verse is based on part of a hymn to the Virgin Mary which is here twisted to become a hymn to Eva. Certainly many of her most fanatical supporters came to regard Eva as little short of a saint during the last days of her illness and after her death, a vision that Peron did not discourage. Official mourning for Eva Peron was extravagant and protracted.

CHE

You let down your people Evita
You were supposed to have been immortal
That's all they wanted
Not much to ask for
But in the end you
Could not deliver

Sing you fools! But you've got it wrong
Enjoy your prayers because you haven't got long
Your queen is dead, your king is through
She's not coming back to you

Show business kept us all alive
Since 17 October 1945
But the star has gone, the glamour's worn thin
That's a pretty bad state for a state to be in

Instead of government we had a stage
Instead of ideas, a prima donna's rage
Instead of help we were given a crowd
She didn't say much but she said it loud

Sing you fools! But you've got it wrong
Enjoy your prayers because you haven't got long
Your queen is dead, your king is through
She's not coming back to you

CROWD

Salve regina mater misericordiae
Vita dulcedo et spes nostra
Salve, salve regina Peron
Ad te clamamus exules filii Eva
Ad te suspiramus gementes et flentes
O clemens O pia

He foresees here that Peron will have difficulty long surviving the death of his wife who had given his regime much of its glamour and inspiration. However it is important when reading or writing about Eva Peron — especially where a work like *Evita* is concerned, which is her story not his, and which does not attempt to deal directly with the political aspects of Peronism or even with Peron's own contribution to their fortunes — not to underestimate the magnetism, drive and ability of Juan Peron.

Nevertheless, the loss of his wife was a crippling political setback to Peron, who had many other problems on his plate by 1952 and he only remained in power for another three years.

17 October 1945 was a great day for the Peronist movement. It was on that date that a huge pro-Peron demonstration took place in the Plaza de Mayo. From fifty to a hundred thousand workers filled the square, calling for Peron, who had been recently deprived of his Ministries (War, and Labour and Welfare) by the far from secure military regime under its third President in two years, General Farrell. It is hard to establish just how much Eva contributed to the organization of this dramatic show of support for her then lover, but she was there or thereabouts in the chaotic days preceding the event. Although Peron was not formally declared President until 4 June 1946 (by which time he had married Eva), it is from 17 October 1945 that his days of power must be reckoned.

As we shall see, Che was far from being the only Argentinian disenchanted with the legend of Eva Peron and sickened by the mindless adulation of Evita by the working masses.

¡SILENCIO!

Not even the many critics of Eva Peron can deny that during her lifetime she was a symbol of hope and success to many Argentinians who had never before had a leader with whom they could identify. There must indeed have been many at the funeral who felt that Eva had died for them and that the extravagant death rites, the lamentations and the cannons, were a tribute to the people too.

THE VOICE OF EVA

Don't cry for me Argentina
For I am ordinary, unimportant
And undeserving
Of such attention
Unless we all are —
I think we all are

Ride on my train O my people
And when it's your turn to die you'll remember
They fired those cannons
Sang lamentations
Not just for Eva
For Argentina
Not just for Eva
For everybody
So share my glory
So share my coffin
So share my glory
So share my coffin

CHE

It's our funeral too

The first appearance of Eva in *Evita* is a post-humous one. These lines are heard by all who mourn her, but is the dead Eva actually there?

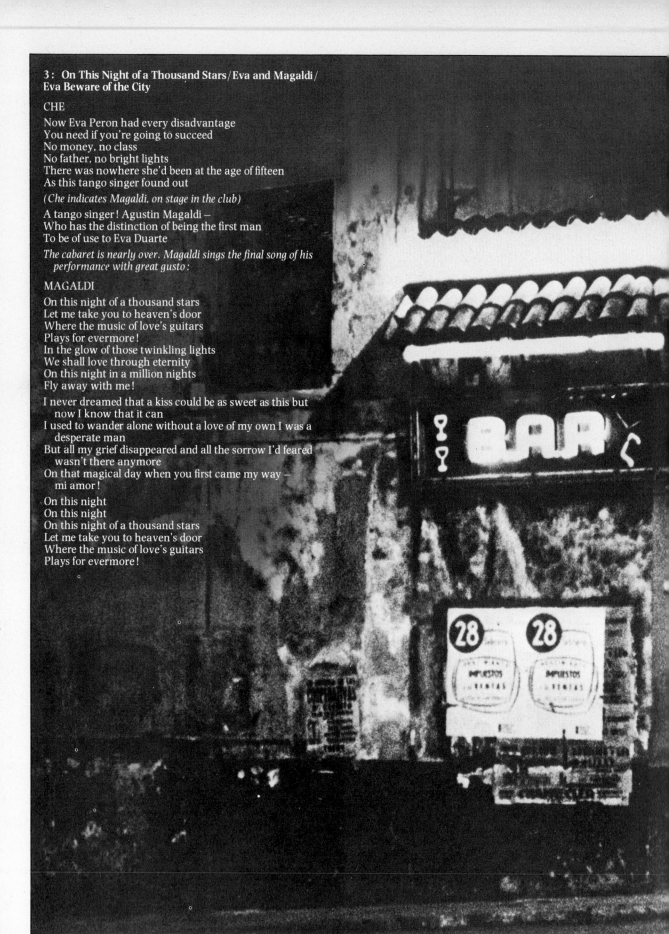

**3: On This Night of a Thousand Stars/Eva and Magaldi/
Eva Beware of the City**

CHE

Now Eva Peron had every disadvantage
You need if you're going to succeed
No money, no class
No father, no bright lights
There was nowhere she'd been at the age of fifteen
As this tango singer found out

(Che indicates Magaldi, on stage in the club)

A tango singer! Agustin Magaldi —
Who has the distinction of being the first man
To be of use to Eva Duarte

*The cabaret is nearly over. Magaldi sings the final song of his
    performance with great gusto:*

MAGALDI

On this night of a thousand stars
Let me take you to heaven's door
Where the music of love's guitars
Plays for evermore!
In the glow of those twinkling lights
We shall love through eternity
On this night in a million nights
Fly away with me!

I never dreamed that a kiss could be as sweet as this but
    now I know that it can
I used to wander alone without a love of my own I was a
    desperate man
But all my grief disappeared and all the sorrow I'd feared
    wasn't there anymore
On that magical day when you first came my way —
    mi amor!

On this night
On this night
On this night of a thousand stars
Let me take you to heaven's door
Where the music of love's guitars
Plays for evermore!

E*vita* now flashes back in time to 1934. The scene is a night club in Junin, Eva's home town at that time. She was born Maria Eva Duarte on 17 May 1919 in Los Toldos, a village 150 miles or so miles west of Buenos Aires. Her father, Juan Duarte, was never married to her mother, Juana Ibarguen, but never allowed the fact that he was married to another woman interfere with his creation of a large family with Juana. There were five illegitimate Duarte children in all, Eva being the youngest. The batting order was two girls, Elisa and Blanca, the only boy, Juan, and finally two more girls, Arminda and Eva.

Agustin Magaldi was a popular tango singer who played Junin in 1934. The only recording by Magaldi in our possession shows his actual work to be somewhat less strident than 'On This Night Of A Thousand Stars' which is a deliberate pastiche of modern Latin-flavoured pop hits. The fifteen-year-old Eva Duarte quickly latched onto this famous entertainer from the glittering city of Buenos Aires.

Tango singer Agustin Magaldi (centre)

Many facts about Eva's early life are now obscure, often as a result of efforts by Eva after she became famous to make herself seem younger, or poorer in childhood, than she actually was, but it is true that the 'unofficial' Duarte family did not always have an easy time. Juan Duarte senior died when Eva was only seven and this event had a momentous effect on Eva, not only because his death greatly worsened her family's financial position, but also because Eva's father's legitimate family (middle class, conservative, landowners) made every attempt to prevent Eva's batch of Duartes from attending or even being seen at Juan Duarte's funeral. Juana and her children were totally ignored by the respectable Duartes from then on. Eva never forgave the middle classes.

Magaldi, as portrayed in *Evita*, was therefore not helping his argument that Eva should not come with him to Buenos Aires by suggesting that it was only a city for the rich or for the middle class. We shall never know just how close the relationship was between the singer and the ambitious teenager from Junin, but since, throughout her life, Eva was never averse to going to extreme lengths in order to get her way, it is reasonable to assume that she did not hold back from giving Magaldi everything she had to give – in other words, he probably seduced her.

Eva (below, far right) enjoyed acting from an early age. Facing page: Eva's mother

Magaldi joins the Duarte family at their table. Che is loitering nearby at the bar.

EVA *(starry-eyed, to Magaldi)*

To think that a man
As famous as you are
Could love a poor little nothing like me . . .

MAGALDI *(to the family in general)*

The audience seemed
Extremely heavy going –

CHE

Listen chum face the fact
They don't like your act

MAGALDI

But this is the sticks!
If this were Buenos Aires
I have that town at my feet
I dare not even meet
Members of the public!
They'd tear me apart –

CHE

I understand their feelings

EVA

I wanna be a part of BA
Buenos Aires – Big Apple!

FAMILY

She wants to be a part of BA
Buenos Aires – Big Apple!

CHE

Just listen to that!
They're onto you Magaldi
I'd get out while you can

EVA

It's happened mama!
I'm starting to get started
I'm moving out with my man

MAGALDI

Now Eva don't get carried away

EVA

Monotony past
Suburbia departed
Who could ever be fond of the back of beyond?

MAGALDI

Don't hear words that I didn't say

FAMILY

What's that? You'd desert the girl you love?

MAGALDI

The girl I love? Who?

FAMILY

She really brightened up your out-of-town engagement
She gave you all she had – she wasn't in your contract
You must be quite relieved that no one's told the papers –
So far

EVA

I wanna be a part of BA
Buenos Aires – Big Apple!
Would I have done what I did
If I hadn't thought –
If I hadn't known
We would stay together?

CHE

Seems to me there's no point in resisting
She's made up her mind, you've no choice
Why don't you be the man who discovered her?
You'll never be remembered for your voice

MAGALDI

The city can be paradise for those who have the cash,
The class or the connections – what you need to make
  a splash
The likes of you get swept up in the morning with the trash
If you were rich or middle class –

EVA

Fuck the middle classes!
I will never accept them
And they will never deny me anything again!
My father's other family were middle class
And we were kept out of sight, hidden from view, at his
  funeral! (*This line sung by Eva and Family*)
If these are the people of Buenos Aires
I welcome the chance to shine in their city
And to trample their rotten values into the ground!

CHE

Do all your one-night stands
give you this trouble?

By 1934, the fortunes of Eva's family had picked up considerably from their rock-bottom position of the time of Juan Duarte's death. Eva's mother ran a boarding-house in Junin. She was not the kind of lady to miss any opportunity to help her children improve their lot. Her two eldest daughters were eventually to marry two of her wealthier lodgers, and when she realized that Eva was obsessed with the theatrical world she gave Eva every encouragement in her attempts to get to the big city, where dreams of being a star had a chance of coming true. Thus she and the rest of her family weighed in heavily against Magaldi's protests that Eva should not go with him to Buenos Aires. ('Big Apple' is of course a nickname for New York City, but the temptation to use the phrase in reference to Buenos Aires was too great to resist and I was thus able to play around with the initials B and A four times in ten words.)

MAGALDI

Eva, beware of the city
It's hungry and cold, can't be controlled – it is mad
Those who are fools are swallowed up whole
And those who are not become
What they should not become:
Changed – in short they go bad

EVA

Bad is good for me. I'm bored, so clean and so ignored
I've only been predictable – respectable!
Birds fly out of here so why
Oh why oh why the hell can't I?
I only want variety of society
I wanna be a part of BA
Buenos Aires – Big Apple!

FAMILY

She wants to be a part of BA
Buenos Aires – Big Apple!

MAGALDI

Five years from now I shall come back
And finally say, you have your way, come to town
But you'll look at me with a foreigner's eyes
The magical city a
Younger girl's city, a
Fantasy long since put down

EVA

All you've done to me – was that a young girl's fantasy?
I played your city games all right – didn't I?
I already know what cooks – how the dirty city feels and
   looks
I tasted it last night – didn't I?
I'm gonna be a part of BA
Buenos Aires – Big Apple!

FAMILY

She's gonna be a part of BA
Buenos Aires – Big Apple!

MAGALDI

Eva beware your ambition
It's hungry and cold – can't be controlled, will run wild
This in a man is a danger enough
But you are a woman, not
Even a woman, not
Very much more than a child and whatever you say
I'll not steal you away!

Looking down the 'Diagonal' to the Plaza de Mayo

4: Buenos Aires

Eva and Magaldi arrive in Buenos Aires — Magaldi lost the argument.

EVA

What's new? Buenos Aires
I'm new — I wanna say I'm just a little stuck on you
You'll be on me too!

I get out here, Buenos Aires
Stand back — you oughta know what'cha gonna get in me
Just a little touch of star quality!

Fill me up with your heat with your noise with your
    dirt overdo me
Let me dance to your beat make it loud let it hurt run it
    through me
Don't hold back you are certain to impress
Tell the driver this is where I'm staying

Hello Buenos Aires
Get this — just look at me, dressed up somewhere to go
We'll put on a show!

Take me in at your flood give me speed give me lights
    set me humming
Shoot me up with your blood wine me up with your
    nights watch me coming
All I want is a whole lot of excess
Tell the singer this is where I'm playing

Stand back Buenos Aires
Because you oughta know what'cha gonna get in me
Just a little touch of star quality!

And if ever I go too far
It's because of the things you are
Beautiful town — I love you
And if I need a moment's rest
Give your lover the very best
Real eiderdown — and silence

*During the orchestral break at this point Che tells a tale of a
    typical day for the Argentine aristocracy*

CHE

On the 9th of February 1935, one of the most important
polo matches of the Buenos Aires season took place

Buenos Aires is now (1978) the fourth largest city in the world with a population of nine million, only Tokyo, Shanghai and Mexico City containing more people. In January 1935, when Eva first hit the city, its population was only in the region of two million but it was even then by far the largest city in South America and the eleventh largest in the world. It has been described by Europeans as a cross between Paris and Barcelona. It is an elegant city laid out in a rectangular pattern, extending back from the river front, the river being the Rio de la Plata, the River Plate. Buenos Aires (the name of the town literally means 'Good Winds') is situated on the west bank of the estuary of the river. Some of the most impressive features of the Argentine capital are the streets themselves, in particular the 425-foot-wide Avenida 9 de Julio, and the Calle Florida, a narrow street with a magnificent variety of shops near the centre of town, now a pedestrian precinct. Many of the cinemas of Buenos Aires were in the Avenida Corrientes — in 1935 the inhabitants of the city were becoming accustomed to the phenomena of national and international film stars, and it was to this aspect of the excitement of Buenos Aires that Eva Duarte was drawn, rather than to its sophisticated business, cosmopolitan, sporting or academic attractions. The contrast between Junin and Buenos Aires must have been striking indeed to her.

The Calle Florida

between a team of leading Argentine players and the touring British side. The home team won, but as the British Ambassador pointed out, the result did not reflect badly on British horsemanship. Three of the Argentine players were Old Harrovians. He refrained from pointing out that the entire Argentine side had had British nannies or governesses.

EVA
You're a tramp you're a treat you will shine to the death
    you are shoddy
But you're flesh you are meat you shall have every breath
    in my body
Put me down for a lifetime of success
Give me credit – I'll find ways of paying

Rio de la Plata! Florida! Corrientes! Neuve de Julio!
All I want to know!

Stand back Buenos Aires
Because you oughta know what'cha gonna get in me
Just a little touch of
Just a little touch of
Just a little touch of star quality!

5: Goodnight and Thank You

CHE

Goodnight and thank you Magaldi
You've completed your task what more could we ask of
  you now
Please sign the book on your way out the door
And that will be all
If we need you we'll call
But I don't think that's likely somehow

EVA

Oh but it's sad when a love affair dies
But we have pretended enough
It's best that we part, stop fooling ourselves

CHE

Which means get stuffed

CHE

Having arrived it matters to be
Photographed, noticed continually

*(Eva is besieged by photographers. Che addresses one particular
  photographer)*

Goodnight and thank you whoever
She's in every magazine, she wouldn't have been on
  her own
We don't like to rush but your case has been packed
If we've missed anything you could give us a ring
But we don't always answer the phone

EVA

Oh but it's sad when a love affair dies
But when we were hot we were hot
I know you'll look back on the good times we've shared

CHE

But Eva will not

s soon as Eva reached Buenos Aires she began her quest to become a successful actress. Magaldi had been invaluable to her in getting her away from Junin, but he seems to have contributed little else towards Eva's slow climb to glory. It took her a very long time to achieve anything of note in Argentine show business despite her iron determination, her many lovers, often men of influence in the entertainment industry, her good looks and adequate acting ability. She was as cynical about her male companions as they were about her. Magaldi soon got the elbow (but for all we know this might not have caused him many sleepless nights – probably just the opposite).

Slowly Eva began to get a few very small parts in theatrical productions. She studied drama (but 'rested' for long periods), and began to get her photographs into magazines.

Eva Duarte was an attractive girl, but not phenomally so. However, right from her earliest days in Buenos Aires, she displayed her talent for making the most of what she had. She was naturally dark and not blessed with a stunning figure. She dyed her hair blonde and even when her opportunities for splashing out on fine clothes were limited, always managed to include some item of originality in her dress which normally won her a second glance from potential admirers or employers. Her greatest asset was her face, and with blonde hair, her dark eyes and full sensuous lips became striking indeed. Eva knew well that a girl who looks as though she knows what sex is all about will attract more men than the innocent-looking one; she cultivated that look for all she was worth.

CHE and EVA

There is no one, no one at all
Never has been and never will be a lover
Male or female
Who hasn't an eye on
In fact they rely on
Tricks they can try on their partner
They're hoping their lover will help them or keep them
Support them, promote them
Don't blame them
You're the same

CHE

Now you are recognized, visually known
You need to move to the microphone

(Eva is besieged by radio men. Che addresses one particular radio man)

Goodnight and thank you whoever
We're grateful you found her a spot on the sound radio
We'll think of you every time she's on the air
We'd love you to stay
But you'd be in the way
So put on your trousers and go

EVA & REJECTED LOVERS

Oh but it's sad when a love affair dies
The decline into silence and doubt
Our passion was just too intense to survive

CHE

For God's sake get out!

Fame on the wireless as far as it goes
Is all very well but every girl knows
She needs a man she can monopolize
With fingers in dozens of different pies . . .

Those who hate Eva Peron state that she was a prostitute at this point in her life (they also believe that Eva's mother's boarding house back in Junin was a brothel). Both these charges are probably unfair – both Eva and her mother were happy to let business arrangements be cemented between the sheets but there is nothing to prove that the business was what happened between the sheets.

The position of women in Argentine society was one of total subservience to men. All but the very rich women – and the very determined women – were doomed to spend their lives as unimportant appendages to males. Few women ever questioned this fact of Argentine life; it never crossed their minds that their situation could, or should, be altered. A woman had no vote, no right to divorce, she and her children and her property were all the property of her husband. She probably had had no choice in the matter of her husband in the first place. Those rare women who did not wish to stay at this level of degradation – such as Eva Duarte – can hardly be blamed if they resorted to drastic action in order to scramble up the ladder, or if they used the male sex the way their own sex had been used for so long. Eva Peron herself was to do much to improve the female's lot when she came to power, both by statute and by example.

Eva got her first part of any significance in a play on Argentine Radio in 1939. About the same time she tried to make some headway in films. However Carole Lombard and Greta Garbo did not have much to worry about – Eva Duarte was not about to set the world, or even Argentina, alight with any movies. In 1941 she appeared in a series of radio dramas sponsored by a soap

company and managed also to persuade the company to employ her brother Juan – not as an actor. These shows went out on Buenos Aires' leading radio station, Radio Belgrano. In 1943 she performed in a series of radio dramas about famous women of the past, including Queen Elizabeth of England, Napoleon's Josephine, Catherine the Great and Lady Hamilton, also for Radio Belgrano. By this time her personal economic position was fairly secure. She installed herself in a comfortable flat in the Calle Posadas close to Radio Belgrano. With her income from her radio work, a lesser income from the few parts she found in films, and the support and attentions of admirers, Eva had come quite a way since her days with Magaldi.

But she was to go a lot further yet! Eva had done everything she could have hoped for when she left Junin in January 1935, but the achieve-ment of her earliest ambitions did not satisfy her – rather it fired her with the desire for more attention, more money, more fame, and for power.

At this point in *Evita*, Che is expressing enthusiasm for Eva's progress – if she can make it from her humble background, surely others can do likewise? The real Guevara probably never looked upon Eva's success story in this way, but plenty of poor Argentinians did – an attitude Eva in power was later to turn to her advantage when she encouraged her followers to identify with the riches and fame she had won, thus justifying (she claimed) her flaunting of luxury and wealth. The real Guevara in fact had a far less deprived start in life than did Eva. His family were middle-class in ambition if not in fact and his father was rarely troubled by the kind of financial crises that hovered around the Duarte homestead.

Eva's first brush with the military was a fictional one, in the early days of her film career

THE OFFICERS OF THE G.O.U. (including PERON)

One has no rules
Is not precise
One rarely acts
The same way twice
One spurns no device
When practising the art of the possible

One always picks
The easy fight
One praises fools
One smothers light
One shifts left to right
It's part of the art of the possible

(Cut to Eva broadcasting)

The first time Peron is seen in *Evita* (unless he is glimpsed at the funeral) he is with his fellow officers of the G.O.U. — of which more later.

Juan Peron was born on 8 October 1895 at Lobos, a town sixty miles south-west of Buenos Aires. Peron's childhood was at times no more privileged than Eva's. His family's fortunes rose and fell. When he was five, they were at a low ebb and the Perons moved way down south to a sheep ranch in Patagonia, barren, cold and sparsely populated — a part of Argentina that resembles the remotest areas of Scotland, except that there is much more of Patagonia. His father was of Sardinian descent (the family name was originally Peroni) and his mother's family in part of Argentine Indian blood.

A few years later, the Peron outlook perked up again and young Juan's family returned to the Buenos Aires area, to another sheep ranch. At school, Peron's talents lay in the athletic rather than academic fields. He gained admission to the Colegio Militar (Military College) in 1911 at the age of sixteen, where he continued to display prowess at sport — riding, boxing, fencing, shooting. He graduated at eighteen from the Colegio Militar as a second lieutenant and proceeded to the Sargento Cabral Officers' School. His graduation from that establishment came in 1924, as a captain. All the while he had jumped into jock-strap, shorts or other sporting apparel, or picked up a sword or pistol, at every opportunity, and with every success. Captain Peron then went to the Superior War School (Escuela Superior de Guerra) where he became Professor of Military History and was appointed to the War Ministry.

Peron wrote four books on military operations during his time as a military student and teacher — *The Eastern Front In the World War of 1914, The*

Theory of Military History, The Russo-Japanese War (three volumes), and *Operations in 1870* (this last work in two volumes and in collaboration with a Colonel of the Argentine General Staff). These books may not have been everybody's bedtime reading but were more than competent publications, regarded at the time as valuable contributions to military bibliography. Peron's knowledge of matters martial became impressively

extensive between the two world wars.

In 1936 he was appointed military attaché in Chile. His next posting abroad took him to Italy, where he was able to witness the political and military tactics of Benito Mussolini from first-hand. He was undoubtedly influenced by the less than subtle tenor of Mussolini's policies and methods of keeping his dictatorial grip on his country. He was not as blind to Il Duce's faults as Che in *Evita* suggests; he was later to say 'We shall create a fascism that is careful to avoid all the errors of Mussolini.' While absorbing aspects of Mussolini, Peron found time to visit other European states, including Hitler's Germany. In Italy he was able to put his sporting skills to good use, taking part in skiing manoeuvres with Italian mountain troops. He introduced skiing to Argentine soldiers in the Andes when he returned home.

Peron married the first of his three wives, Aurelia Tizón, a schoolteacher, in 1928. In 1938 Aurelia died. There has often been speculation that Peron had children by his first wife (neither of his two subsequent marriages produced any) and indeed while Peron was in exile in Spain before his final return to Argentina in 1972, a lady emerged in Buenos Aires calling herself Lucia Virginia Peron, claiming to be the daughter of Juan Peron, born to his first wife in 1936.

Peron's sexual exploits are a subject about which it is hard to be precise. There are those who claim he would leap onto anything that moved of either sex, and those who maintain that he had interests only in certain specialized areas of carnal activity. The truth is probably that Peron was a man of normal sexual drive whose position of power afforded him ample opportunity to indulge in a variety of bedtime companionship that lesser mortals only dream of knowing. It does seem however that Peron liked them young. His mistress at the time Eva came into his life was a girl of only sixteen, and many of Peron's other women were a good deal younger than he was. He was 24 years older than Eva, and 35 years senior to his third wife, Isabel.

In 1936, after elections of the most doubtful honesty, Roberto M. Ortiz became President of Argentina. Ortiz, a man of gigantic physical proportions, had the backing of the military who wanted him to be nothing more than a tubby figurehead. Ortiz however was an honest man, and because of this surprising fact, on becoming President began to investigate and to clean up the widespread corruption that had flourished under his predecessor, President Justo. This was not what the army had ordered; nor were they the only enemies Ortiz thus created for himself. Ortiz wanted to work towards the establishment of a genuine social democracy — the civilian establishment felt that they too had much to lose should the lower classes be allowed greater privileges and participation in Argentina's affairs and prosperity.

Ortiz was not a healthy man and in 1940 the condition of this man of great bulk and great integrity deteriorated to the point where he had to hand over control to Vice President Ramon S. Castillo, who was aggressively anti-democratic. In theory, Ortiz was still President, but in practice the conservative oligarchy and the military were now at the helm via Castillo, with no united radical opposition to trouble them.

President-elect Roberto M. Ortiz (left) on his way to take the oath of office, accompanied by Ramon S. Castillo

Peron came back to Argentina as power was passing from Ortiz to Castillo and his supporters. In the continent he had just left the Second World War had begun. Victory for Hitler seemed inevitable. Fired with enthusiasm for the Nazi cause, inspired by Hitler's megalomaniac plans to lead, to conquer all of Europe, Peron saw the future of Argentina in South America as a parallel to that of the Third Reich in Europe. Peron was not alone in dreaming these dreams; even those officers of his generation in the Argentine army who had not personally witnessed the European dictators in action had a similar vision. Only the military could bring glory to Argentina;

civilians could not even comprehend the ideal.

Against this background, a society of officers was formed, named the Grupo de Oficiales Unidos (Group of United Officers) who stood for Government, Order and Unity. Peron was a key figure in the founding of the G.O.U. which by 1943 included the vast majority of officers in the Army. By now Castillo was President in his own right, but while his corrupt regime posed no threat to the well-being of the military, his civilian government clearly did not have the ability or ambition to lead the nation towards greater things. A manifesto issued that year by the G.O.U. made no secret of the group's aims; only a military dictatorship controlling every aspect of the lives of all Argentinians — their newspapers and radio programmes, their religion and their education — could fulfil the country's glorious destiny. 'Hitler's fight in peace and war will be our guide' they stated.

On 4 June 1943, the G.O.U. met little resistance from Castillo. The army marched in, Castillo and his cabinet ran out, and General Ramirez emerged as the new President. Peron became chief of the Secretariat of the War Ministry. He was now an important public figure. One of the people who began to take a great interest in him was Eva Duarte.

Eva had just about established herself as a fully professional radio performer at the time of the arrival of Peron and the G.O.U. on the political stage. After the coup her circle of acquaintances began to change — the army were the boys to know now. The man appointed Minister of Posts and Telegraphs, in charge of the nation's entire broadcasting network, was Colonel Imbert. Eva's attentions soon left her soap manufacturer / sponsor / lover and switched to Imbert, no Adonis but obviously the most useful of the men of power for a radio actress to cultivate. Once a hanger-on of military society she was able to see where the real power lay — not with President Ramirez, but in the hands of a fairly small group of colonels. One of the most immediately interesting of these was Colonel Juan Peron, already spoken of as the strong man among the colonels.

There are plenty of stories that exist about Eva's exploits with the military in the months after the 4 June 1943 take-over. It is said that she boldly telephoned President Ramirez and invited herself out to dinner with him, which led to a liaison between the two; it is said that she broadcast long tributes to the genius of Peron before she had ever met him; that she had affairs with nearly every soldier of political importance. The stories relating to nearly every period of her life became more bizarre and more exaggerated after her death (this is a problem many legends have to face) but as far as the latter half of 1943 is concerned one can say that this was the time when she first entertained serious ambitions beyond success in show business, that she would not hesitate to lie to or lie with anyone to achieve them, and that her ability to hitch her fortunes to the correct rising star attracted her in particular to Juan Peron.

EVA

I'm only a radio star with just one weekly show
But speaking as one of the people I want you to know
We are tired of the decline of
Argentina with no sign of
A government able to give us the things we deserve

(Back to the officers)

*The armed coup in June 1943 put the G.O.U. firmly in control
of Argentina's future*

eron's philosophy for political survival was always a cool, calculated step ahead of the majority of his cynical colleagues. He was the first to realize that the regime could not long survive without support from outside the military. While other officers made less subtle plans to topple Ramirez from his perch, Peron set about obtaining the support of a vast and untapped source of power – the workers, organized labour. He obtained a position as Director of the National Labour Department which later in 1943 became elevated to the Secretariat of Labour and Public Welfare.

The fateful moment when Eva Duarte first met Juan Peron cannot be positively identified. There is evidence to suggest that they met as early as September 1943 but the most likely date is 22 January 1944. They were finally brought together by an earthquake which had devastated the Argentine town of San Juan in the north of the country. It was a truly shattering disaster – 3,500 killed and 10,000 injured – and if it was indeed the event that introduced the two most ambitious people in Argentina to each other, its tremors are still being felt today.

Eva, still with broadcasting supremo Imbert at this point, immediately took up a prominent position in show-business efforts to raise money for the surviving victims of the earthquake. There is no reason to doubt her genuine sympathy for the cause, but it is certain that Eva was more than alert to the opportunity the charity work gave her to sparkle in the spotlight, as she had never done before. She pleaded for the homeless over the radio, she collected money in the streets, she displayed reserves of efficiency and energy which were remarkable. The climax to the campaign was a huge rally and concert at Luna Park Stadium in Buenos Aires. The leaders of Argentina's entertainment world, including the fast-rising Eva Duarte, were there in force. So were the leaders of Argentina's government, including the fast-rising Juan Peron.

Eva attended the concert with Imbert as her escort, but by the end of the evening he had joined the long list of Eva Duarte's former lovers.

Agustin Magaldi could well have been there too.

Peron too had used the San Juan tragedy to best advantage. His new Ministry of Labour and Welfare set up a Relief Fund for the wrecked town. Suddenly Peron was everywhere, caring for the people whose lives had been thrown into chaos and despair. His noble deeds were written about in the newspapers and spoken of on the radio, not least by Eva Duarte – even before she ever met him. Whether any of the very large sum of money collected by his Ministry ever actually got to San Juan was of little importance to Peron compared with the boost his apparently charitable activities gave to his own reputation with the working class.

OFFICERS

One always claims
Mistakes were planned
When risk is slight
One takes one's stand
With much sleight of hand
Politics is the art of the possible

EVA (*on the air — she is very emotional, perhaps a little too emotional*)

I still feel destroyed by the news from San Juan
By the earthquake that has now taken over three
   thousand lives
But at last I can tell you how you can help the injured
   and survivors
The leaders of the government and of the entertainment
   world have organized a concert in aid of the victims
I want you all to come
I pray that you will all come

(*Back to the officers*)

OFFICERS

One has no rules
Is not precise
One rarely acts
The same way twice
One spurns no device
In politics — the art of the possible

7: Charity Concert/I'd Be Surprisingly Good for You

*Magaldi is finishing his spot in the concert held in aid of
   victims of the San Juan earthquake.*

MAGALDI

On this night
On this night
On this night of a thousand stars
Let me take you to heaven's door
Where the music of love's guitars
Plays for evermore!

(*Crowd applauds wildly. Magaldi goes off stage. He immediately runs into Eva*)

Eva Duarte!

EVA

Your act hasn't changed much

(*She turns away from him*)

MAGALDI

Neither has yours

(*Peron pushes past, leaps onto stage. Crowd noise surges to
   new level of enthusiasm*)

PERON

Tonight I'm proud to be the people's spokesman!
You've given help to those who've lost their homes
But more than that , conclusively shown
The people should run their affairs on their own
Make sure your leaders understand the people!

(*The crowd begin to chant 'Peron, Peron'. Peron leaves the
   stage with the sound of his own name ringing in his ears.
   Now Peron confronts Eva for the first time. She has been
   applauding him too*)

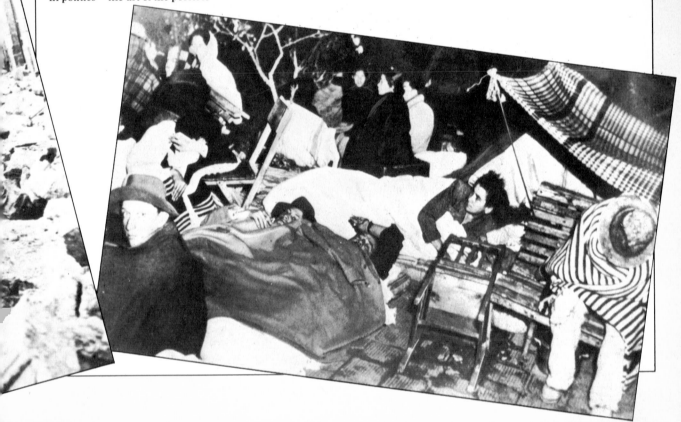

EVA

Colonel Peron?

PERON

Eva Duarte?

EVA & PERON

I've heard so much about you!

EVA

I'm amazed! For I'm only
    an actress
Nothing to shout about
Simply a girl on the boards
But when you act
The things you do affect us all

PERON

I'm amazed! For I'm only
    a soldier
One of the thousands
Defending the country he
    loves

PERON

But when you act, you take us away from the squalor of
    the real world
Are you here on your own?

EVA

Yes, Oh yes

PERON

So am I
What a fortunate coincidence
Maybe you're my reward for my efforts here tonight

EVA

It seems crazy but you must believe
There's nothing calculated, nothing planned

Please forgive me if I seem naive
I would never want to force your hand
But please understand
I'd be good for you

I don't always rush in like this
Twenty seconds after saying hello
Telling strangers I'm too good to miss
If I'm wrong I hope you'll tell me so

But you really should know
I'd be good for you
I'd be surprisingly good for you

I won't go on if I'm boring you
But do you understand my point of view?
Do you like what you hear, what you see and would you be
Good for me too?

I'm not talking of a hurried night
A frantic fumble then a shy goodbye
Creeping home before it gets too light
That's not the reason that I caught your eye
Which has to imply
I'd be good for you
I'd be surprisingly good for you

PERON

Please go on — you enthrall me!
I can understand you perfectly
And I like what I hear, what I see, and knowing me
I would be good for you too

EVA

I'm not talking of a hurried night
A frantic tumble then a shy goodbye
Creeping home before it gets too light
That's not the reason that I caught your eye
Which has to imply
I'd be good for you
I'd be surprisingly good for you

EVA & PERON (though neither seems aware that the other
    is singing)

There is no one, no one at all
Never has been and never will be a lover, male or female
Who hasn't an eye on
In fact they rely on
Tricks they can try on their partner
They're hoping their lover will help them or keep them
Support them, promote them
Don't blame them, you're the same

(Eva and Peron leave together)

Peron might well have heard a good deal about Eva Duarte, but probably through army gossip and as a result of her aggressive work for the earthquake fund, rather than because of her acting talents. His immediate interest in her could not have been anything more than sexual attraction.

Eva's beeline for Peron was certainly calculated and planned — she wanted him because no other man in the country could have been more help to her wild aspirations. At the same time she found Peron, then in his forty-ninth year, a highly attractive man with whom she had much in common in that he too had clawed his way towards the top of the heap from a highly unpromising start in life. Later, when the Perons were installed in the Presidential Palace, Eva would recall with monotonous regularity that their relationship was forged by their mutual hatred of injustice and their common love of the people. Not so of course; but while it may not have been true love, it is not true to say that they felt nothing for each other.

Before Peron's initial desire for the vivacious actress had time to wear off, he realized that in Eva Duarte he had a woman who could give him much more than his previous bed-mates. She flattered him, she encouraged his belief that he was to be the next great leader of his country, she told her radio audiences of his genius.

Eva had been aware of what Peron could do for her before their relationship began — once Peron became aware of what she could do for him it was inevitable that their liaison would last.

Immediately prior to his introduction to Eva, Peron's most favoured female companion had been a girl of no more than sixteen. (On occasions he attempted to pass her off as his daughter.) It was not difficult for a hustler such as the 24-year-old Eva Duarte to turf this unfortunate teenager out of Peron's apartment and out of his life. A more sophisticated mistress would have been no match for Eva either. Peron and Eva set up home together in the Calle Posadas, in an apartment next door to the one Eva had until then occupied.

8: Another Suitcase in Another Hall

Peron's flat. Eva bursts in to throw Peron's 16-year-old mistress out.

EVA *(almost affectionately)*

Hello and goodbye!
I've just unemployed you
You can go back to school
You had a good run
I'm sure he enjoyed you
Don't act sad or surprised
Let's be friends, civilized
Come on little one!
Don't stand there like a dummy!
The day you knew would arrive
Is here – you'll survive
So move, funny face!

I like your conversation – you've a catchy turn of phrase
You're obviously going through some adolescent phase
Maybe you've got something more than just a pretty face
Maybe not –

(Eva has by now bustled the mistress out)

Outside in the hall:

MISTRESS

I don't expect my love affairs to last for long
Never fool myself that my dreams will come true
Being used to trouble I anticipate it
But all the same I hate it – wouldn't you?
So what happens now?

CHE & CHORUS

Another suitcase in another hall

MISTRESS

So what happens now?

CHE & CHORUS

Take your picture off another wall

MISTRESS

Where am I going to?

CHE & CHORUS

You'll get by you always have before

MISTRESS

Where am I going to?

Time and time again I've said that I don't care
That I'm immune to gloom that I'm hard through and
   through
But every time it matters all my words desert me
So anyone can hurt me – and they do
So what happens now?

CHE & CHORUS

Another suitcase in another hall

MISTRESS

So what happens now?

CHE & CHORUS

Take your picture off another wall

MISTRESS

Where am I going to?

CHE & CHORUS

You'll get by you always have before

MISTRESS

Where am I going to?

Call in three months' time and I'll be fine I know
Well maybe not that fine but I'll survive anyhow
I won't recall the names and places of this sad occasion
But that's no consolation here and now.
So what happens now?

CHE & CHORUS

Another suitcase in another hall

MISTRESS

So what happens now?

CHE & CHORUS

Take your picture off another wall

MISTRESS

Where am I going to?

CHE & CHORUS

You'll get by you always have before

MISTRESS

Where am I going to?

CHE & CHORUS

Don't ask any more

9: Peron's Latest Flame

CHE

At the watering-holes of the well-to-do
I detect a resistance to

ARISTOCRATS

Precisely!

CHE

Our heroine's style

ARISTOCRATS

We're glad you noticed

CHE

The shooting sticks of the upper class —

ARISTOCRATS

Give her an inch . . .

CHE

Aren't supporting a single arse
That would rise for the girl

ARISTOCRATS

. . . She'll take a mile

Such a shame she wandered
Into our enclosure – how
Unfortunate this person
Has forced us to be blunt
No we wouldn't mind
Seeing her in Harrods
But behind the jewellery counter
Not in front

Argentine economic development took off in a big way at the beginning of the twentieth century. Foreign funds poured into Argentina primarily from Europe and in particular from Great Britain. By 1912 many of the more than one million square miles of this vast country had been developed agriculturally; ploughed, sown with alfalfa and cereals, fenced in for pasture. Pedigree bulls and rams were imported to improve the local breeds. 20,000 miles of railway had been built by this date, a network of windmills across the pampas pumped water to the surface for the huge numbers of livestock.

The British influence was great. In all but name Argentina was a colony of Britain. The railways that had opened up the country were British; the trams, telegraphs, telephones, electricity, freezers (vital for the refrigeration of meat exports) were all British. The drainage systems and water works, which rid the country of yellow fever, and the country's banking system were British developments. British clubs, newspapers, social customs and sport (cricket flourished and horse racing was a major item in the social calendar) all took root seven thousand miles away from their homeland. There still is a Harrods department store in the Calle Florida. All this despite the fact that over three-quarters of the population is of Spanish or Italian descent, the national language being Spanish.

The country was rich, but the wealth remained in the hands of very few. Furthermore Argentina depended so much upon Britain and Europe for export of its meat and grain that when these markets were virtually closed for the duration of each of the two world wars it became apparent that industry would have to be developed in order that the country could achieve some degree of economic independence. By 1944, times were changing, but an examination of the lives of the monied upper class would not have made one think so. They continued to ape the between-the-wars life-style of Europe's rich, sending their children to Britain for education, taking holidays in Paris and Rome.

Convinced that the sources of their riches and superiority were inexhaustible, that the peasantry now working in the new factories and those pouring into Buenos Aires to seek a new kind of job would behave as the agricultural peasantry always had, the landed aristocracy of Argentina lived as though their power, money and privilege were sacred and unassailable. Small wonder then that the continuing presence of Senorita Duarte in their rarefied circles annoyed them.

In 1946, following an Anglo-Argentine trade agreement, Peron became a 'City butcher'. Elected an Honorary Freeman of the Worshipful Company of Butchers of the City of London, here he signs the Company's diploma

So far the ultra-conservative oligarchy had no reason to regard Eva as a major threat — they saw her as a jumped-up harlot, a tasteless nuisance. Elements of the military were the first to have genuine reason to resent Eva's attachment to Peron.

CHE

Could there be in our fighting corps
A lack of affection for —

ARMY

Exactly!

CHE

Peron's latest flame?

ARMY

You said it brother

CHE

Should you wish to cause great distress
In the tidiest officers' mess
Just mention her name

ARMY

That isn't funny

The man is a fool breaking every taboo
Installing the girl in the army H.Q.
And she's an actress! The last straw
Her only good parts are between her thighs
She should stare at the ceiling not reach for the skies
Or she could be his last whore
The evidence suggests
She has other interests
If it's her who's using him
He's exceptionally dim

ARISTOCRATS

We have allowed ourselves to slip
We have completely lost our grip
We have declined to an all-time low
Tarts have become the set to know

ARMY

It's no crime for officers to do as they please
As long as they're discreet and keep free from disease
We ignore, we disregard
But once they allow a bit on the side
To move to the centre where she's not qualified
We should all be on our guard
She should get into her head
She should not get out of bed
She should know that she's not paid
To be loud but to be laid

Gentlemen of the army were never worried about the sexual exploits of their colleagues, but the apparent infatuation of Colonel Peron with Eva Duarte did affect them. Eva showed no respect for their rank, nor for their male superiority. So quickly and so thoroughly did Eva identify with every aspect of Peron's life that she treated his friends, acquaintances and enemies the way he did, only more so. It was hard to avoid her — she was at his side virtually everywhere he went, and as the atmosphere of intrigue and plotting that existed in the G.O.U. at the time necessitated many important meetings taking place in secret at Peron's apartment Eva was often present at the scenes of most crucial political scheming. It was hard, too, for other officers to know which of Peron's actions were inspired by Peron himself and which by Eva; at this point in their lives Eva in fact instigated very few of Peron's moves and made very little contribution to his decisions, but so vocal and dynamic was she in her support for everything Peron said or did that it must have seemed to many that she was providing the ideas as well as the enthusiasm.

All this suited Peron perfectly. He had a truly remarkable supporter working for him in his aim to become the soldier who finally emerged as the man in command of Argentina. Eva was making herself indispensable to Peron which suited her perfectly because she knew he would become President before long — with her help.

Eva's career as an actress took off like a rocket after she set up home with Peron. Managers of radio stations now appeared desperate to give work – and highly paid work, too – to Colonel Peron's close friend. Not only did Eva take leading roles in radio plays, she also broadcast regularly on current affairs programmes, lecturing her listeners on topics such as Patriotism and Motherhood, and of course on the valiant work of Peron and his Ministry of Labour and Welfare. Even in films Eva began to succeed. At last she was being given big parts in pictures, which she had never been offered before. Her photograph appeared in show-business magazines, each time more prominently. Soon she was featured in all kinds of newspapers and magazines, the subject of many interviews. She was now earning a lot of money on top of the material support Peron gave her and her appearance reflected her improved financial state. She dyed her hair blonde. Her wardrobe was extensive, her jewellery and perfumes extravagant and sophisticated.

Yet although she was now doing all the things she had set out to do when she left Junin nearly ten years before, and although her success in show business had been as spectacular as she

CHE (*in the guise of a reporter*)

This has really been your year Miss Duarte
Tell us where you go from here Miss Duarte
Which are the roles you yearn to play
Whom did you sleep – dine – with yesterday?

EVA (*the glamorous movie star, protected by two heavies*)

Acting is limiting, the lines not mine
That's no help to the Argentine

CHE

Can we assume then that you'll quit?
Is this because of your involvement with Colonel Peron?

HEAVIES (*pushing Che aside and Eva out*)

Goodnight and thank you

ARMY

She won't be kept happy by her nights on the tiles
She says it's his body but she's after his files
So get back onto the street!
She should get into her head
She should not get out of bed
She should know that she's not paid
To be loud but to be laid

ARISTOCRATS

Things have reached a pretty pass
When someone pretty lower class
Graceless and vulgar, uninspired
Can be accepted and admired

could have hoped for a decade earlier, she was dissatisfied. She was already more interested in the even more fantastic opportunities that could come her way via the most influential lover she had ever had. She enjoyed the show-biz glory for a while, the chance to crow over all those who had never recognized her acting potential, the chance to settle scores with radio and film producers who had ignored her for so long – but through Peron she was tasting the excitement of the political stage, and this she found even more stimulating.

The political scene in Argentina during the time of Eva's dizzy rise to stardom was a turbulent one, even more unsettled and traumatic than that of the previous few years. Dramatic event followed dramatic event in a constant stream of confusion; it was hard for anyone to remain ahead of the game; even Peron and Eva at one time lost nearly everything they had. The end result of this bewildering sequence of happenings was that Juan Peron emerged as the man who had managed to fight his way to the top of the sordid pile – by the time he got there factions within the army and the aristocracy had even more reason to hate Eva.

10: A New Argentina

1945. No secure leader has emerged from the group of officers who seized power in 1943. Peron has the support of the workers and because of this the strongest movement within the military heirarchy is an anti-Peron feeling rather than one pro-anybody else.

PERON

Dice are rolling, the knives are out
I see every bad sign in the book
And as far as they can – overweight to a man!
They have that lean and hungry look

EVA

It doesn't matter what those morons say
Our nation's leaders are a feeble crew
There's only twenty of them anyway
What is twenty next to millions who
Are looking to you?
All you have to do is sit and wait
Keeping out of everybody's way
We'll
You'll be handed power on a plate
When the one who matter have their say
And with chaos installed
You can reluctantly agree to be called

PERON

There again we could be foolish
Not to quit while we're ahead
For distance lends enchantment
And that is why
All exiles are distinguished
More important, they're not dead
I could find job satisfaction in Paraguay

WORKERS' VOICES

Peron! Peron!

EVA

This is crazy defeatist talk
Why commit political suicide?
There's no risk, there's no call for any action at all
When you have unions on your side

Eva, above with miners, fought hard for the support of the workers. After less than a year in office, President Ramirez (left) was replaced by Colonel Farrell (right) in 1944

The military government that had booted Castillo out in June 1943 gradually became less and less stable. In early 1944, President Ramirez was forced out of office by the G.O.U., after he had capitulated to public opinion and broken off relations with Nazi Germany, and was replaced by Colonel Edelmiro Farrell. This was shortly after the San Juan earthquake and Eva's first meeting with Peron.

Farrell made Peron Minister of War. The importance of this post coupled with Peron's ever-increasing control of organised labour meant that he was indisputably the most powerful man in the country. Peron (and Eva) were now waiting for the right moment to make their move, working to build a position of such strength that their hold on the Presidency would not be as brief as that of recent incumbents.

Inevitably, Peron's actions during these final hectic months leading up to his triumph won him more and more enemies within the military regime; opposition to him and to Eva grew as they inched closer to their goal. Eva was never more valuable to Peron than she was at this time. When moments of crisis came to them, it was Peron who was always ready to give some consideration at least to the soft option, to the abandonment of their plans, if that was the only way they could guarantee their personal safety. Eva never once lost sight of her objective; having sunk her teeth into the flesh of real power, she never let go. Perhaps the difference between them was that Peron put his own skin before everything else; Eva put nothing whatsoever before her desire for power, not even her own skin.

There were certainly moments before 17 October 1945 when Peron considered running away. When he was actually separated from Eva in the early part of that crucial October he even requested in writing of his captors that he be allowed to go into exile. (However while they were apart Eva was working frantically amongst the unions and she was ultimately able to produce Peron's finest hour for him at the eleventh hour.)

Ten years after these events, in 1955, Peron did sample exile – which lasted for a further seventeen years – and during that time away from Argentina, his stature in his own country rose from rock-bottom to that of a saviour, while he did nothing at all. He not only became more distinguished in the eyes of his people but also stayed alive.

Peron as Secretary of Labour and as Minister of War was in a powerful position behind the throne. When Farrell made Peron Vice President (there was no other possible candidate) the addition of this post to the two other offices gave Peron all the political clout he needed to manipulate those he wished to use in order to fulfil his ultimate ambitions.

Peron's tactics at this time were extremely unpleasant. While he publicly championed the cause of the hitherto downtrodden Argentine worker, union leaders who were not sympathetic to his cause were locked up or disappeared and were replaced by leaders who were. Newspapers which did not fall in line were closed down. Radio stations were not able to broadcast criticism. This last item was Eva's province in particular and she was in her element spouting pro-Peron propaganda over the airwaves. Those who went on strike or threatened to cause any form of dissent within the workers' ranks also found themselves in prison. There were reports of the torture of some of these uncooperative people, which were often horrifyingly accurate. No one who voiced the wrong opinions loudly was safe — workers, teachers, lecturers, churchmen.

Yet the vast majority did not see or understand what was really happening; as Peron intended, they only saw the public Peron who was the first politician they had known who had fought for them. They did not see Peron's syndication of the various independent unions into one great bloc entitled the Confederation General de Trabejo (C.G.T.) as a device that would give Peron a tighter grip on every type of workers' organization; they noted only their increased wages which this wonderman was arranging for them.

Eva's position in the radio world was of course a great asset to Peron. She was beginning to attract a following in her own right. For the first time in her life her performances at the microphone could be described as brilliant — as she reminded her audiences that she too was a worker for whom Peron was the answer to everything.

Dolan Getta is a fictitious name for the union leader in *Evita*. We cannot really recall why we did not use the name of a real union man such as Cipriano Reyes, the meat workers' leader, an important Peronist in 1945, who none the less fell foul of the Perons within three years and eventually joined many others who had done the same — in gaol.

DOLAN GETTA *(A union leader)*

A new Argentina!
The chains of the masses untied!
A new Argentina!
The voice of the people
Cannot be denied!

EVA

There is only one man who can lead any workers' regime
He lives for your problems, he shares your ideals and
    your dream
He supports you for he loves you
Understands you, is one of you
If not, how could he love me?

GETTA & MOB

A new Argentina!
The old one has gone sadly wrong
A new Argentina!
The voice of the people
Rings out loud and long!

EVA

Now I am a worker I've suffered the way that you do
I've been unemployed and I've starved and I've hated it too
But I found my salvation
In Peron — may the nation
Let him save them as he saved me

Vice President Peron appointed Colonel Filomeni Velazco chief of the Buenos Aires police force. Even by the standards of the average Peron henchman, Velazco was an unsavoury gentleman. Enemies of Peron who could not be persuaded to abandon their opposition often came to know Velazco well. His police dispensed with details such as evidence when making arrests, which were on many occasions the prelude to torture.

Peron was already stirring up a crude form of warped patriotism among the working class by implying that the foreign investment and interests in Argentina had much to do with their misfortunes. He was to rework this theme to maximum effect during his presidential election campaign in 1946, when he found a perfect foreign enemy of Argentina in the U.S. Ambassador.

Farrell's regime slumped to a new low in the popularity stakes in September 1945. A huge protest march against the government took place in Buenos Aires, encompassing every kind of opposition from Communist to Conservative. It was clear even to the G.O.U. that the Argentine people, ashamed of their leaders' association with the defeated Axis Powers, would not tolerate any longer the state of siege that had been imposed upon the country's constitution since the presidency of Castillo. But a return to general elections would give Peron the opportunity he needed to move in for the kill — he would obviously be a candidate for the presidency in any campaign, despite his claims to the contrary.

SECRET POLICE

A new Argentina!
A new age about to begin!
A new Argentina!
We face the world together
And no dissent within!

(*They club an unfortunate dissenter*)

GETTA

Nationalization of the industries
That the foreigners control
Participation in the profits that we make
Shorter hours, higher wages
Votes for women, larger dole
More public spending, a bigger slice of every cake

PERON

It's annoying that we have to
Fight elections for our cause
The inconvenience – having to get a majority
In normal methods of persuasion
Fail to win us applause
There are other ways of establishing authority

SECRET POLICE (*laying into another victim*)

We have ways of making you vote for us, or at least of
     making you abstain

EVA

Peron has resigned from the army and this we avow
The descamisados are those he is marching with now!
He supports you for he loves you
Understands you – is one of you
If not – how could he love me?

GETTA/MOB/EVA/PERON/SECRET POLICE

A new Argentina!
The chains of the masses untied!
A new Argentina!
The voice of the people
Cannot be
And will not be
And must not be
Denied!

Peron's many enemies within the military therefore used the violent protest from the people as an opportunity to eliminate Peron from the scene. Almost as important to the G.O.U. was the elimination of Eva, whose influence in matters political had been further boosted by the appointment (by Peron) of her own friends and relations to important posts in government and government-related offices. They therefore demanded Peron's resignation (and that of his chief of police, Velazco) with the aim of satisfying public clamour for a political shake-up with the announcement that the Vice President, Minister of War and Secretary for Labour and Welfare had quit.

They were able to make this announcement on 10 October. We cannot be certain whether Peron's resignation was a brilliantly subtle move or sheer cowardice in the face of disagreeable threats, but his withdrawal from the front line meant that of the two forces he had cultivated over the years his immediate future lay with the workers, not with the army. No one saw this more clearly than Eva.

'Descamisados' literally means 'shirtless ones', a description of the workers originally intended to imply an insult, but transformed by Eva into a term of glory. Eva's descamisados were usually coatless rather than shirtless.

Juan Peron's first brief fall from power was in early October 1945, when the G.O.U. used the strikes and protests sweeping Argentina as an excuse to remove him from the Vice-Presidency

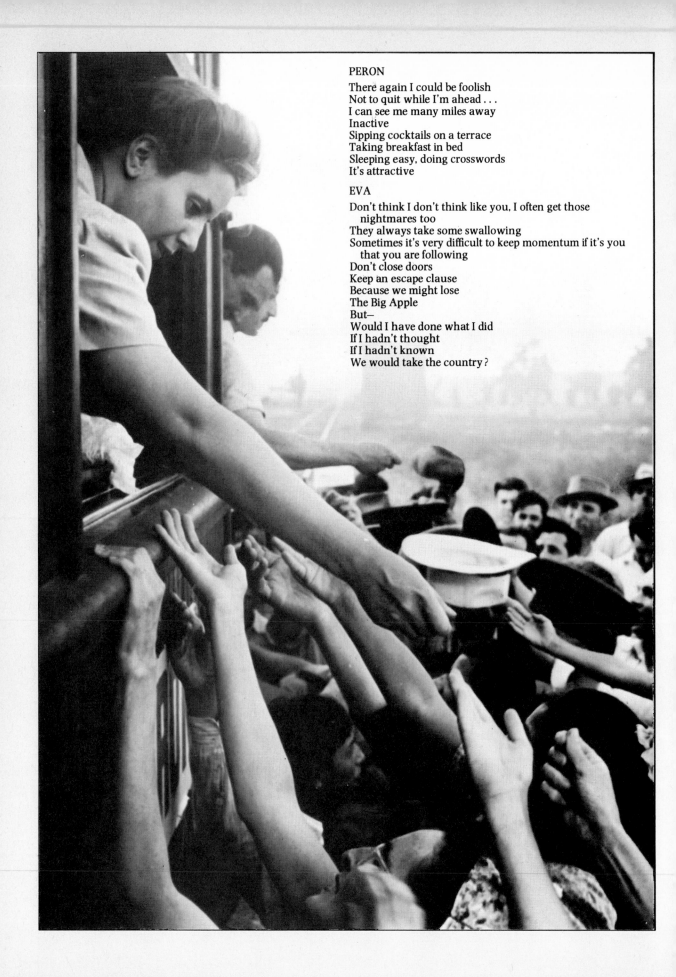

PERON

There again I could be foolish
Not to quit while I'm ahead . . .
I can see me many miles away
Inactive
Sipping cocktails on a terrace
Taking breakfast in bed
Sleeping easy, doing crosswords
It's attractive

EVA

Don't think I don't think like you, I often get those
    nightmares too
They always take some swallowing
Sometimes it's very difficult to keep momentum if it's you
    that you are following
Don't close doors
Keep an escape clause
Because we might lose
The Big Apple
But—
Would I have done what I did
If I hadn't thought
If I hadn't known
We would take the country?

The seven days between Peron's resignation and his triumphant return to the balcony of the Casa Rosada on 17 October were frantic and confused.

Once Peron had been designated official government scapegoat, it became prudent for him and Eva to leave their apartment, and indeed the city, which was now witnessing some spectacular anti-Peron demonstrations. They moved out to Tres Bocas, a resort on the Rio de La Plata, but were almost immediately brought back to Buenos Aires where Peron was put under arrest. Peron under arrest did not present such a bold face to the world as had Peron the tyrant at large with his union and police support. He claimed he was ill, he asked to be allowed to go into exile, which he may well have been contemplating even before his arrest.

Crisis, on the other hand, brought out the best in Eva. While she was prepared, as a last resort, to accept a deal (if one could be struck) with the military that would enable Peron to be released from prison if they both left the country, she set her sights a good deal higher than that on behalf of her beleaguered lover.

With sensational energy, Eva set about amassing as much support from the unions as possible. She visited factories, the docks, union headquarters, demanding help for the man who had only the descamisados' interests at heart and was now suffering for them. She was helped in her crusade by the chaotic state of all potential opponents — of Farrell's government, and of the opposition parties, who could not, or would not, unite, even temporarily, to present the people with a credible democratic opposition to the army. Anti-Peron demonstrations were not the only noises on the streets and the government did not help their cause by their brutal treatment of most disturbances, even ones against Peron.

Eva had cash (San Juan earthquake funds?) and friends — Cipriano Reyes was the union leader most valuable to her. She and the influential head of the meat packers' union began to organize a demonstration to end the uncertainty of Argentina's crisis of leadership.

Peron's work over the previous year and a half in creating one huge union of unions (the C.G.T.) now paid off; when Eva was able to get this body's official declaration of support for Peron, her battle was virtually won. 17 October was the great day — more than 50,000 workers poured into the Plaza de Mayo and howled for Peron. Farrell and his gang had little choice; they not only set Peron free but announced he had never been arrested in the first place. On the balcony of the Casa Rosada Farrell embraced Peron and Peron delivered an emotional tribute to his descamisados.

Peron's groundwork in 1944–45 had contributed to his success; the confusion and incompetence of his enemies had too; but nothing had been of greater help to him than Eva.

A few days after 17 October, Peron and Eva were married. There remained just one final step in the staggering climb of Eva Duarte from unknown small-town girl to world-famous political personality, and this she took on 4 June 1946, when Peron was sworn in as President. Eva had become the First Lady of Argentina.

Eva had thrown herself into the election campaign with (at least) one hundred per cent enthusiasm. Her trips with Peron to areas outside Buenos Aires were often pure show biz. She paraded before the people in her wonderful jewels and clothes; she scattered gifts and peso notes to the crowds that clamoured to catch a glimpse of this striking lady who, marvellous to relate, was of humble origin like themselves. She represented everything the poor and underprivileged had ever dreamed of being. She was the perfect all-purpose image: mother, wife, local girl, sophisticated lady, even saint. Eva made the most stunning of impressions upon many whose lives were devoid of excitement and without purpose or variety. It was hardly surprising that, even at this early stage of her public life, the more simple of her followers in the more remote areas of the country would begin to equate, or to confuse, her image with that of the only other extraordinary female image they knew — that of the Virgin Mary. They called her 'Evita' now.

During the campaign, when Peron had toured or had otherwise been seen with his wife, he had been content to play the role of handsome husband at the side of a glamorous semi-saint. On other occasions he had preferred a part he was more used to — that of dishonest and violent political animal.

The rival presidential candidate had been Dr José Tamborini, a radical, representing the combined opposition to Peron's Labour Party. Once more the forces against Peron had lacked cohesion and organization, in no state to cope with the Peronist tactics. Riots and damage, shootings and terrorism had followed Tamborini nearly everywhere he had campaigned; the vile Velazco had been returned (by Peron) to his position at the head of the government police force. The outgoing President Farrell had been totally in Peron's pocket.

Voting had taken place on 24 February 1946. Peron won 1·5 million votes to Tamborini's 1·2 million. Not an overwhelming victory, but a victory that Peron could claim was the democratic judgement of the Argentine people.

Eva's acting career was now abandoned — or was it?

Juan Peron speaking to his supporters, marrying Eva, and receiving the mace and sash of office from retiring President Farrell on 4 June 1946. Bottom right, Dr José Tamborini

11: On The Balcony of the Casa Rosada / Don't Cry For Me Argentina

Peron has just won the 1946 Presidential Election. This is the first public appearance by Peron and Eva, now married, since Peron's triumph. Action takes place both inside and on the balcony of the Casa Rosada.

OFFICER NO. 1 (on the balcony)

People of Argentina! Your newly elected president — Juan Peron!

CROWD (in the square below)

Peron! Peron!

PERON (*coming out onto the balcony*)

Argentinos! Argentinos!
We are all shirtless now! (*He removes his jacket and rolls up his shirt sleeves*)
Fighting against our common enemies
      Poverty
      Social Injustice
      Foreign domination of our industries
Reaching for our common goals
      Our independence
      Our dignity
      Our pride
Let the world know that our great nation is re-awakening
And that its heart
Beats in the humble bodies
Of Juan Peron — and his wife
The First Lady of Argentina, Eva Duarte de Peron!

CROWD (*even more enthusiastically*)

Peron! Peron!

CHE (*in crowd*)

As a mere observer of this tasteless phenomenon
One has to admire the stage management

(*Heavies move in on Che*)

There again perhaps I'm more than a mere observer!
Listen to my enthusiasm gentlemen!
Peron! Peron!
Look! If I take my shirt off, will you . . .

(*Heavies bundle Che away. The crowd begin to change their chant from 'Peron' to 'Evita'*)

CROWD

Evita! Evita!

EVA *(coming out onto the balcony)*

It won't be easy, you'll think it strange
When I try to explain how I feel
That I still need your love after all that I've done
You won't believe me
All you will see is a girl you once knew
Although she's dressed up to the nines
At sixes and sevens with you

I had to let it happen; I had to change
Couldn't stay all my life down at heel
Looking out of the window, staying out of the sun
So I chose freedom
Running around trying everything new
But nothing impressed me at all
I never expected it to

Don't cry for me Argentina
The truth is I never left you
All through my wild days
My mad existence
I kept my promise
Don't keep your distance

And as for fortune, and as for fame
I never invited them in
Though it seemed to the world they were all I desired
They are illusions
They're not the solutions they promised to be
The answer was here all the time
I love you and hope you love me

Don't cry for me Argentina —

(Eva breaks down; the Crowd take up her tune)

EVA

Don't cry for me Argentina
The truth is I never left you
All through my wild days
My mad existence
I kept my promise
Don't keep your distance

Have I said too much? There's nothing more I can think
 of to say to you
But all you have to do is look at me to know that every
    word is true

She acted superbly.

(Eva goes back inside, out of sight of the crowd who are cheering ecstatically)

Just listen to that!
The voice of Argentina!
We are adored! We are loved!

OFFICER NO. 2
Statesmanship is more than entertaining peasants

EVA
We shall see, little man

CROWD

Evita Peron! La Santa Peronista!

(Eva goes back onto the balcony)

EVA

I am only a simple woman who lives to serve Peron in his noble crusade to rescue his people!
I was once as you are now!
I have taken these riches from the oligarchs only for you — for all of you!
One day you will inherit these treasures!
Descamisados! When they fire those cannons, when the crowds sing of glory, it is not just for Peron, but for all of us! All of us!

(Eva goes back inside)

ARISTOCRATS

Things have reached a pretty pass
When someone pretty lower class
Can be respected and admired —

EVA

But your despicable class is dead!
Look who they are calling for now!

Eva did not actually deliver any major oration on the day of Peron's inauguration but it was not long before Argentina's new First Lady was making highly emotional speeches of the intensity we hope we have hinted at in 'Don't Cry For Me Argentina'. Once she stepped away from the spotlight she was capable of an instant change of personality, particularly when confronted with her old adversaries, but this does not mean that her performances to her followers were totally insincere.

One can only guess how much of the content of the dramatic tirades Eva delivered to Argentina from 1945 to 1952 she herself believed.

The driving force behind her insatiable desire for power was revenge, and revenge in particular against the Argentine aristocracy who still refused to accept her — even though she was married to the President. Her protestation of love for her class and for the people who, like her, had been dealt a pretty rotten hand at the start of their lives, was probably more heartfelt than her professed worship of Peron. She wanted to achieve great things for her unprivileged supporters, but her motive was not simply a passionate desire for social justice.

As her megalomania increased, as the events in her amazing life steam-rollered from one excess to another, and as her following became more and more extravagant and more and more divorced from logic and reality, she must have found it hard to know exactly what it was she did believe in; but she never lost her compelling, magic authority at the microphone or on the platform, whatever it was she might be saying, for whatever motive.

Her justification of her flamboyant display of wealth — that she was wearing the jewels of the oligarchs for her beloved descamisados — was accepted with delight by her disciples.

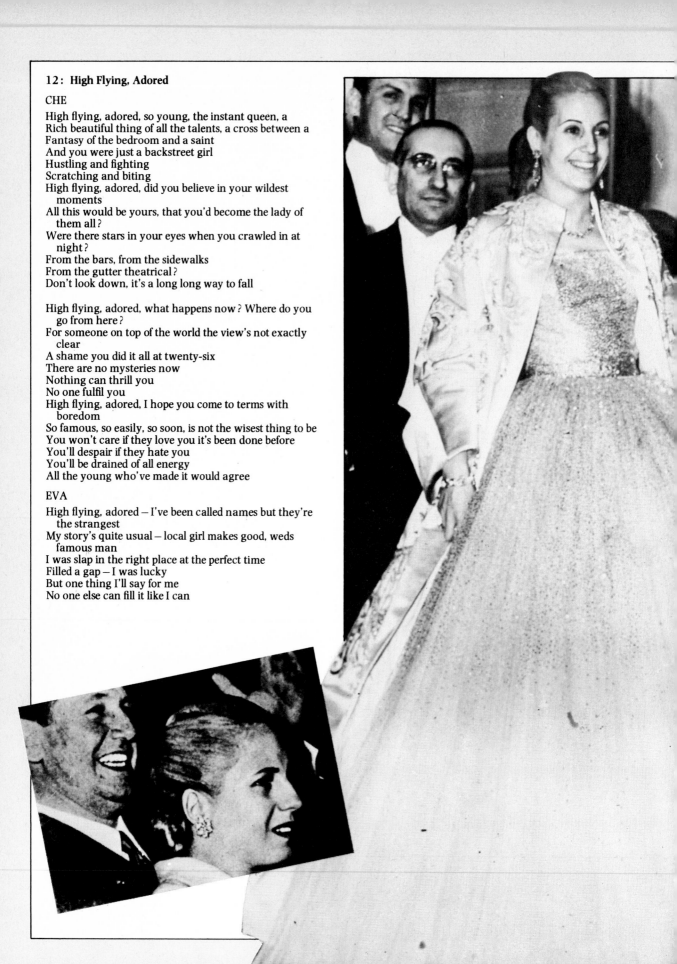

12: High Flying, Adored

CHE

High flying, adored, so young, the instant queen, a
Rich beautiful thing of all the talents, a cross between a
Fantasy of the bedroom and a saint
And you were just a backstreet girl
Hustling and fighting
Scratching and biting
High flying, adored, did you believe in your wildest
    moments
All this would be yours, that you'd become the lady of
    them all?
Were there stars in your eyes when you crawled in at
    night?
From the bars, from the sidewalks
From the gutter theatrical?
Don't look down, it's a long long way to fall

High flying, adored, what happens now? Where do you
    go from here?
For someone on top of the world the view's not exactly
    clear
A shame you did it all at twenty-six
There are no mysteries now
Nothing can thrill you
No one fulfil you
High flying, adored, I hope you come to terms with
    boredom
So famous, so easily, so soon, is not the wisest thing to be
You won't care if they love you it's been done before
You'll despair if they hate you
You'll be drained of all energy
All the young who've made it would agree

EVA

High flying, adored — I've been called names but they're
    the strangest
My story's quite usual — local girl makes good, weds
    famous man
I was slap in the right place at the perfect time
Filled a gap — I was lucky
But one thing I'll say for me
No one else can fill it like I can

13: Rainbow High

EVA

I don't really think I need the reasons why I won't
    succeed – I have done!
Let's get this show on the road
Let's make it obvious
Peron is off and rolling

HAIRDRESSERS / BEAUTY CONSULTANTS / FASHION
   DESIGNERS

Eyes! Hair! Mouth! Figure! Dress! Voice! Style!
Movement! Hands! Magic! Rings! Glamour! Face!
Diamonds! Excitement! Image!

EVA

I came from the people
They need to adore me
So Christian Dior me
From my head to my toes
I need to be dazzling
I want to be rainbow high!
They must have excitement
And so must I

HAIRDRESSERS etc.

Eyes! Hair! Mouth! Figure! Dress! Voice! Style! Image!

EVA

I'm their product!
It's vital you sell me
So Machiavell-me
Make an Argentine Rose!
I need to be thrilling
And I shall be rainbow high
They need their escape
And so do I

HAIRDRESSERS etc.

Eyes! Hair! Mouth! Figure! Dress! Voice! Style!
Movement! Hands! Magic! Rings! Glamour! Face!
Diamonds! Excitement! Image!

EVA

All my descamisados expect me to outshine the enemy –
    the aristocracy
I won't disappoint them
I'm their saviour!
That's what they call me
So Lauren Bacall me
Anything goes
To make me fantastic
I have to be rainbow high
In magical colours
You're not decorating a girl for a night on the town!
And I'm not a second-rate queen getting kicks with a
    crown!

Next stop will be Europe!
The Rainbow's gonna tour
Dressed up, somewhere to go – we'll put on a show!
Look out mighty Europe!
Because – you oughta know what'cha gonna get in me
Just a little touch of
Just a little touch of
Argentina's brand of
Star quality!

Eva in a Dior creation

Eva not only made every effort, sparing no expense, to present the most lavish and exciting image possible to her public, she wasted no time in establishing her influence in several other ways. Her first steps in this direction were taken by means of that good old stand-by, nepotism.

Many of her relations were given positions of authority in the country. Her brother Juan became Peron's private secretary. Lovers and husbands of her sisters and mother were created a Senator, Governor of the province of Buenos Aires, Director of Posts and Telegraph, Director of Customs, and one eventually a judge of the Supreme Court. Through her family alone Eva therefore had

Eva's brother, Juan Duarte

Christian Dior – the Parisian fashion designer who dominated world fashion for a decade after the Second World War. His sensational 'New Look' was launched on 12 February 1947. Eva's Rainbow Tour to Europe began in June 1947.

Machiavelli – the Italian statesman and writer, born in Florence in 1469 whose acute understanding of human nature and of politics resulted in such works as The Prince which stated without compromise what governments have to do in order to govern and to survive. His genius has often unfairly been regarded as the genius of the Devil. He died in 1527.

Lauren Bacall – her distinguished acting career was already well under way by 1947. She filmed The Big Sleep in 1944, and married Humphrey Bogart in 1945.

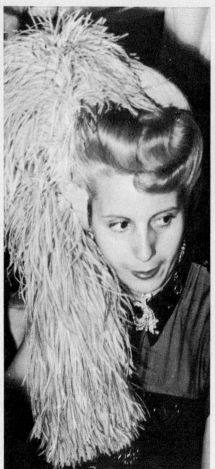
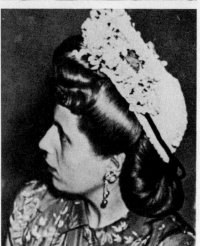

direct access to Argentina's communications, to the provincial government, to her husband's daily schedule, to the Senate and to the judiciary. Only the military were untroubled by Duarte infiltration; the army Eva left for Peron to cope with as best he could – not even her feminine wiles had any hope of cutting much ice there.

Eva's skills were always seen at their best in the field of public relations. Her self-promotion was brilliant; she had filled out and was more attractive at 27 years of age than at any other time in her life. She made the most of her good looks – she could afford to.

Never for a moment did Eva contemplate adopting the traditional role of a president's wife – that of being a decorative appendage to the man of power. She was decorative all right but never a mere accessory to Peron.

One sure way she felt she could hurt the hated oligarchs was to conquer Europe with her stunning personality. Every year the Argentine aristocracy and socialites would dally a while in Europe, keen to impress each other and European society. Eva would outshine them all.

Eva's proposed tour of Europe – the Rainbow Tour – was something that Peron was only too happy to support. Both Perons saw the trip as a superb opportunity for the regime to gain respectability in the Old World, to bury the Nazi Germany/Argentina associations, to re-open the great market in Europe for Argentine meat and grain. Eva saw her visit as a passport to acceptance and respectability all over the world; the Pope and all the leaders of Europe were bound to receive Argentina's Rainbow with enthusiasm and friendship. It is not known whether Peron was happy to be deprived of his wife for several weeks.

150,000 descamisados waved goodbye to her at the airport. Eva's departure was another wildly excessive, emotional affair. A monumental amount of money was spent on every aspect of Eva's tour – on clothes, on the luxurious style of travel, on the army of servants, sycophants and companions who travelled with her (including her brother). It has not been officially stated whence came the small fortune needed to finance the enterprise.

14: Rainbow Tour

PERON

People of Europe! I send you the Rainbow of Argentina!

Eva's plane (which had been totally refitted to suit Eva's exorbitant requirements) landed in Spain to an ecstatic welcome – 200,000 people including General Franco and his wife turned out to greet her.

Any description of the fantastic reception Eva received everywhere in Spain would be an understatement – she could do no wrong and was given every kind of honour, pomp and ceremony that Spain, under a government not dissimilar to that of Argentina and desperately keen to purchase Argentine wheat, could lay on. Her impact on rich and poor alike was staggering.

She moved on to Italy, feeling invincible.

Eva was greeted by General Franco on arrival in Madrid. During her triumphant week in Spain, she was presented by the General with the Grand Cross of Isabel the Catholic, and (above right) attended a bullfight

OFFICER No. 1

Spain has fallen to the charms of Evita
She can do what she likes it doesn't matter much
She's a new world Madonna with the golden touch
She filled a bullring — forty-five thousand seater
But if you're prettier than General Franco
That's not hard

OFFICERS Nos. 1 & 2

Franco's reign in Spain should see out the forties
So you've just acquired an ally who
Looks as secure in his job as you

OFFICER No. 1

More important, current political thought is
Your wife's a phenomenal asset
Your trump card

ALL *(Including Peron & Che)*

Let's hear it for the Rainbow tour
It's been an incredible success
We weren't quite sure, we had a few doubts

OFFICER No. 2

Would Evita win through?

ALL

But the answer is — yes!

(Cut to Eva, still in Europe, but in contact with Peron in Buenos Aires)

EVA

There you are I told you so
Makes no difference where we go
The whole world over — just the same
You should have heard them call our name
And who would underestimate the actress now?

PERON

I'm not underestimating you — just do the
same thing in Italy please

In Italy her progress was not so triumphant. There were crowds at the airport, but only 15,000. Officials of the government met her, but not the Premier. The Spanish Embassy made her feel more welcome in Italy than most Italians did. Although she was granted an audience with the Pope, the Church did not push any boats out for her, giving her a rosary, and a decoration for Peron — not for Eva herself.

The story of Eva and the Italian Admiral is supposed to be true, but there were many such tales flying around about her European venture, not all of which could have been entirely accurate.

In Italy, Eva could be seen leaving an audience with Pope Pius XII (top right), visiting Genoa (top, far right) and Rome's catacombs (bottom right), and attending an opera at La Scala in Milan (bottom left)

OFFICER No. 2

I don't like to spoil a wonderful story
But the news from Rome isn't quite as good
She hasn't gone down like we thought she would

OFFICERS Nos. 1 & 2

Italy's unconvinced by Argentine glory

OFFICER No. 2

They equate Peron with Mussolini
Can't think why

(Cut to Eva in Italy)
EVA

Did you hear that?
They called me a whore!
They actually called me a whore!

EVA'S ITALIAN ESCORT, an EX-ADMIRAL

But Signora Peron
It's an easy mistake — I've had that trouble too
I'm still called an admiral
Yet I gave up the sea long ago

(Back to Peron's office)

OFFICER No. 1

Things aren't all that bad she met the Pope
She got a Papal decoration and a kindly word

OFFICERS Nos. 3 & 4

So even if the crowds gave our lady the bird
The Argentine-Italy axis does have some hope

OFFICER No. 3

Still made a fabulous impact
Caught the eye

ALL *(Including Peron and Che)*

Let's hear it for the Rainbow Tour
It's been an incredible success
We weren't quite sure, we had a few doubts

OFFICER No. 1

Would Evita win through?

ALL

But the answer is —

CHE

A qualified —

ALL

Yes!

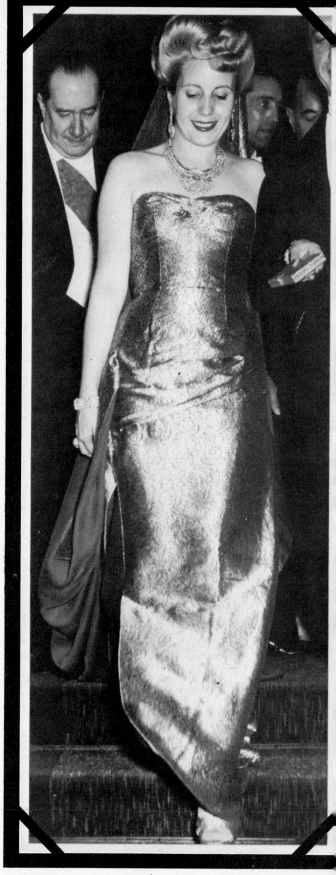

Paris, rather than the capital cities of Spain and Italy, was the second home (literally) of many of Eva's wealthy Argentine opponents. Eva took more care than ever in France to create an impression of majesty and beauty, of a goddess arrived from a distant golden land of plenty.

The French were impressed by her appearance but did not take her political pretensions at all seriously. She was present at the signing of a treaty whereby Argentina loaned France £9 million to help the French post-war reconstruction, but none of the French officials thought it necessary for her to be present when the Argentine Ambassador's signature was available. To the French, she was a beautiful and interesting woman, not a significant international figure.

She soon seemed to weary of the often flippant treatment she got from some Parisians and drifted away to the South of France (where she spent one relaxed day with Aristotle Onassis) and thence to Switzerland, where she is said to have opened her notorious numbered bank account. In Switzerland, a country fairly unaffected by the ravages of the Second World War, her car was stoned and her dress spattered with tomatoes. The Swiss could afford to be open in expressing their opinion of the Peronist regime.

Ablaze with diamonds, Eva made a striking figure as she arrived at a reception held at the Latin American House in Paris on 21 July. She was met on arrival in France by Georges Bidault (above), the French Foreign Minister, and visited President Vincent Auriol and his wife (top, middle) at Rambouillet

OFFICER No. 5

Eva started well, no question, in France
Shining like the sun through the post-war haze
A beautiful reminder of the carefree days
She nearly captured the French, she sure had the chance
But she suddenly seemed to lose interest
She looked tired

ALL

Tired? Evita tired?

*(A general buzz of
reaction to this
news)*

Eva's biggest disappointment on her Rainbow Tour was Britain's refusal to entertain her. She was convinced that she would be given an official invitation to come to London by Attlee's Labour government or by King George VI, but this never materialized, although she made it clear that she would be more than happy to go to Buckingham Palace. The best she got was an unofficial invitation to tea with the Queen, which she turned down, infuriated.

Eva returned home via Rio de Janeiro, where she was made to feel welcome by the Argentine community, if not by the Brazilians themselves, and Uruguay, where she made the briefest of stops — too many Argentinians who had fled across the Rio de la Plata to escape Peron were around in Montevideo to make her stay there comfortable.

The final leg of her long journey was a short sea voyage from Montevideo to Buenos Aires. The crowds that turned out to meet the ship that was bringing Evita home again were as large and as vocal as they had been when she left them two and a half months before. But during her absence Eva had not lost any enemies either.

She turned completely against all things British upon her return to Argentina — and she had not exactly been pro-Britain before. The royal snub cost the many British interests in Argentina dearly, even though in many cases the ejection of the British harmed the Argentines themselves. Britons in every walk of life were told they were not wanted in Argentina — with one minor exception. No home-grown football referees could be found who could withstand bribes and other local pressures. Peron eventually had to re-import British referees in order to save the game, a near-religion in Argentina.

A solemn Eva Peron with her husband and Sir John Balfour, British Ambassador to Argentina, at a reception aboard the Eva Peron after the steamship's maiden voyage from England. After her return home from her Rainbow Tour (right), she had turned against all things British

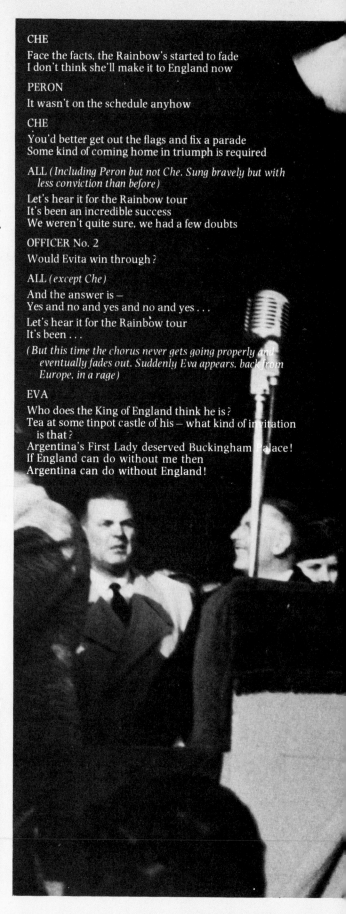

CHE
Face the facts, the Rainbow's started to fade
I don't think she'll make it to England now

PERON
It wasn't on the schedule anyhow

CHE
You'd better get out the flags and fix a parade
Some kind of coming home in triumph is required

ALL (*Including Peron but not Che. Sung bravely but with less conviction than before*)

Let's hear it for the Rainbow tour
It's been an incredible success
We weren't quite sure, we had a few doubts

OFFICER No. 2
Would Evita win through?

ALL (*except Che*)
And the answer is —
Yes and no and yes and no and yes . . .
Let's hear it for the Rainbow tour
It's been . . .

(*But this time the chorus never gets going properly and eventually fades out. Suddenly Eva appears, back from Europe, in a rage*)

EVA
Who does the King of England think he is?
Tea at some tinpot castle of his — what kind of invitation is that?
Argentina's First Lady deserved Buckingham Palace!
If England can do without me then
Argentina can do without England!

15 : The Actress Hasn't Learned (The Lines You'd Like to Hear)

ARISTOCRACY

Thus all fairy stories end
Only an actress would pretend
Affairs of state are her latest play
Eight shows a week (two matinées)
My how the worm begins to turn
When will the chorus girl ever learn?
My how the worm begins to turn
When will the chorus girl begin to learn?

EVA

The chorus girl hasn't learned the lines you'd like to hear
She won't go scrambling over the backs of the poor to be
  accepted
By making donations – just large enough – to the correct
  charity
She won't be president of your wonderful societies of
  philanthropy
Even if you asked her to be
As you should have asked her to be
The actress hasn't learned the lines you'd like to hear
She won't join your clubs
She won't dance in your halls
She won't help the hungry once a month at your tombolas
She'll simply take control as
You disappear

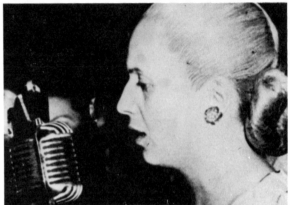

It was a different Eva that returned to Argentina. She realised that she had not impressed the Argentine establishment by her European jaunt and that she probably would not have done even if the tour had been roses all the way. In fact there was probably nothing she could do anywhere that would change the upper classes' attitude towards her. She now abandoned any pretence of trying to. If they would never forgive her for her background, for her time as Peron's mistress, and for her success since her marriage, so be it.

It was customary for the wife of the President of the country to become the honorary President of the Society of the Ladies of Benevolence, a huge, plodding, honest, conservative charitable concern which certainly raised money for deserving causes, but not without raising a good deal of exclusive entertainment and social excitement at the same time for its aristocratic members. The Ladies broke with custom and did not ask Eva to be their President. Eva's response to this decision was the launching of one of the most bizarre organizations that has ever been seen on this planet, the Eva Peron Foundation, designed to eclipse every other charity in Argentina.

CHE

Forgive my intrusion but fine as those sentiments sound
Little has changed for us peasants down here on the
     ground
I hate to seem churlish, ungrateful, I don't like to moan
But do you now represent any cause here but your own?

EVA

Everything done will be justified by my Foundation!

EVA'S STAFF

Goodnight and thank you whoever
We've no time for you
But one thing we do
Want to say
Everyone now gets a crack of the whip
Things may seem bad
To one Argentine lad
But they're bad in a much fairer way

The post-Rainbow Tour Eva was no longer greatly concerned with matters outside the country. Her work was inspired by three causes (in addition to any personal neuroses): her Foundation; the Peronista Feminist Party; and continued, greater, control of the Labour movement via the Secretariat of Labour and Social Welfare, Peron's old hunting ground.

Gradually Eva's physical appearance began to change. While she never lost any interest in the power and acquisition of vast sums of money, she became less ostentatious about it. The jewels and exotic dresses were not seen so often — if things did not actually improve for her followers then there would be a limit to the length of time they would tolerate the sight of money draped around even her body — and she shifted her image to that of the workers' comrade, caring little for personal wealth and comfort when she had so much work to carry out for her people. The change to the austere look was however a slow one and only became complete towards the end of her life.

*T*here are a thousand remarkable stories that could be told about Eva's Foundation, an organization that started out, at least in part, as a spiteful assault on established charities, and with 500 dollars 'out of Eva's own pocket'. By 1952, the year of her death, its income was estimated to be equal to one-third of the entire Argentine national budget, in the region of one hundred million dollars.

Cash flowed into the Foundation in a variety of ways but there was usually an element of compulsion involved. No person or company in the nation who had two pesos to rub together was able to avoid making a contribution at one time or another – or at one time and another. In the early days of the Foundation a few large companies found that they were out of business shortly after refusing to respond to Eva's request for money – in the later days of the Foundation these refusals were much more rare.

The foundation paid no tax, received one-fifth of the profits from the national lottery, extracted 'voluntary' contributions from the unions, from big business and from the stock exchange.

It was as much an exercise in public relations for the Perons as it was a charity. Every good deed was publicized in the Peron-controlled press – every institution or appeal set up by the Foundation glorified the generosity of the Foundation's selfless chief, to whom every person in every corner of the giant bureaucratic empire it had become was responsible. The formula that Eva and Peron had used before to simplify the control of a large number of people (lumping them all together into one massive body when they had formed the C.G.T. back in 1944) worked again.

But let it not be said that the Foundation gave nothing back to Argentina. Schools, hospitals, clinics, even holiday camps were built in large numbers. Those hit by natural disasters received financial aid. Many deprived people benefited from Foundation donations and from Eva's generosity although at times what was good news for one Argentinian was bad for another; for example, there were cases of landlords being made homeless when their property was handed over lock, stock and barrel to their tenants whom Eva considered to have been exploited. Many Foundation gifts were simply gimmicks to draw attention to the good works of Eva Peron. Exceedingly poor children were removed from their destitute surroundings, stuffed with every kind of edible goodie, weighed down with a load of presents, and then flung back into poverty after a few days of the good life. Peso notes were tossed at random into crowds; people were asked to write their names on pieces of paper and the few pieces that Eva's aides grabbed won the owners of the names thereon some kind of bonanza from the Foundation. It was often welfare by lottery and there was little chance of any permanent Welfare State emerging from Eva's chaotic magnanimity.

But all the same, the Foundation could look back on many positive achievements by 1952. Eva often worked eighteen hours a day on Foundation matters, driven on, she said, by her passionate desire to eliminate poverty in Argentina. This may well have been a sincere statement, but the slapdash running of the entire venture coupled with the fact that there were too many motives besides charitable ones for its existence in the first place, meant that the Foundation had little hope of becoming a permanent solution to the nation's social problems.

Eva never kept any accurate records of the Foundation's financial transactions, maintaining that the distribution of the money to those who needed it was more important than counting how much she gave away, and that she did not have time to do both.

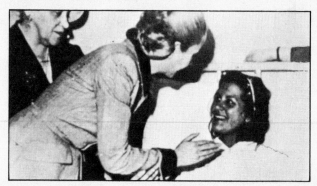

16: And the Money Kept Rolling In (and Out)

Che, having been given the total brush-off by Eva's staff, is now nearly knocked over by the sudden arrival of the Manager of the Eva Peron Foundation and his many minions.

THE MANAGER *(& workers on choruses)*

And the money kept rolling in from every side
Eva's pretty hands reached out and they reached wide
Now you may feel it should have been a voluntary cause
But that's not the point my friends
When the money keeps rolling in you don't ask how
Think of all the people gonna see some good times now
Eva's called the hungry to her – open up the doors!
Never been a fund like the Foundation Eva Peron!

Rolling rolling rolling
Rolling on in

Would you like to try a college education?
Own your landlord's house, take the family on vacation?
Eva and her Blessed Fund can make your dreams come
    true
Here's all you have to do
Write your name and your dream on a card or a pad
    or a ticket
Throw it high in the air and should our lady pick it
She will change your way of life for two whole weeks
    at least!
Name me anyone who cares as much as Eva Peron!

Rolling rolling rolling
Rolling on in
Rolling on out

And the money kept rolling out in all directions
To the poor, to the weak, to the destitute of all
    complexions
Now cynics claim a little of the cash has gone astray
But that's not the point my friends
When the money keeps rolling out you don't keep books
You can tell you've done well by the happy grateful looks

Accountants only slow things down, figures get in the
    way
Never been a lady loved as much as Eva Peron!

Rolling rolling rolling
Rolling on out

17: Santa Evita

CHILDREN

Please, gentle Eva
Will you bless a little child?
For I love you
Tell Heaven I'm doing my best
I'm praying for you
Even though you are already blessed
Please mother Eva
Will you look upon me as your own?
Make me special
Be my angel
Be my everything wonderful perfect and true
And I'll try to be exactly like you
Please holy Eva
Will you feed a hungry child?
For I love you
Tell Heaven I'm doing my best . . .

CHE

Get them while they're young Evita, get them while they're
    young!

CHILDREN

I'm praying for you
Even though you are already blessed

WORKERS

Santa Santa Evita
Madre de todos los ninos
De los tiranisados
De los descamisados
De los trabajadores
De la Argentina

*(This chorus is repeated and fades gradually away as the
    workers and children march off)*

CHE

Why try to govern a country when you can become a
    saint?

I always thought my country right or wrong
I used to say hey here's where I belong
But that's a joke
I might as well have been
As loyal to
El Salvador, Afghanistan, the South of France, Japan,
    Hong Kong!

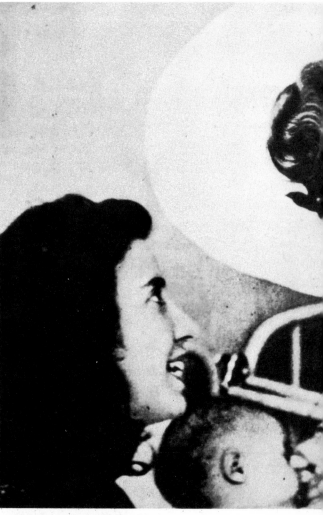

No one was too young to be ignored by Eva in her quest for love and popularity.

The near-deification of Eva did not really get under way until the last few months of her life when she was obviously seriously ill, but as we have already seen, the image of Eva Peron as Santa Evita, the closest thing to the Virgin Mary this side of Heaven, had worked its way into the minds of many of her descamisados from her earliest days of fame.

18 : Waltz for Eva and Che

CHE

Tell me before I waltz out of your life
Before turning my back on the past
Forgive my impertinent behaviour
But how long do you think this pantomime can last?
Tell me before I ride off in the sunset
There's one thing I never got clear
How can you claim you're our saviour
When those who oppose you
Are stepped on or cut up or simply disappear?

EVA

Tell me before you get onto your bus
Before joining the forgotten brigade
How can one person like me, say
Alter the time-honored way the game is played?
Tell me before you get onto your high horse
Just what you expect me to do
I don't care what the bourgeoisie say
I'm not in business for them but to give my
   descamisados
A magical moment or two

There is evil
Ever around – fundamental
System of government quite incidental
So why go bananas
Chasing Nirvanas
And failing?
Better to do
What you can for a few
Than to lie – much
Plainer sailing

CHE

Tell me before I seek worthier pastures
And thereby restore self-esteem
How can you be so short-sighted
To look never further than this week or next week
To have no impossible dream?

EVA

Allow me before you slink off to the sidelines
To mark your adieu with three cheers
And to ask you just who'd be delighted
To know that I'll tackle
The world's greatest problems
Say war to pollution
No hope of solution
Even if I live for one hundred years?

There is evil
Ever around – fundamental
System of government quite incidental
So go if you're able
To somewhere unstable
And stay there
Whip up your hate
In some tottering state
But not here dear
Is that clear, dear?

(Che storms out)

Oh what I'd give for a hundred years!
But the physical interferes
Every day more – oh my Creator!
What is the good of the strongest heart
In a body that's falling apart?
A serious flaw
I hope You know that . . .

In this sequence of *Evita*, the 'Waltz For Eva and Che', we have attempted to portray the truly private Eva, for once shown to be giving an honest account of her philosophy, and for once defending her actions with her true feelings. She may well have believed everything she expected her public to believe, but her public utterances cannot have been her only thoughts.

Prominent among those whose sinister disappearance Che laments here was the reputable and long-established newspaper *La Prenza*, always highly critical of Peronism, which the Perons finally suppressed in 1951 after a long fight with the owners, the Paz family. There were other individuals and enterprises which met similar fates.

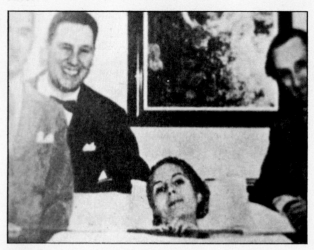

By the middle of 1951, Eva's health was in obvious decline. At first she refused to consent to any medical examination or to make any cuts in her punishing work schedule. It was not until she collapsed shortly after her renunciation of the Vice-Presidential ticket for the elections due to be held in November that she underwent internal examination. Cancer of the uterus was suspected.

*R*ight until the end of Eva's career, the army maintained its total disapproval of their leader's wife. The clash between Eva and the military reached a dramatic climax during the saga of Eva's bid for the Vice Presidency.

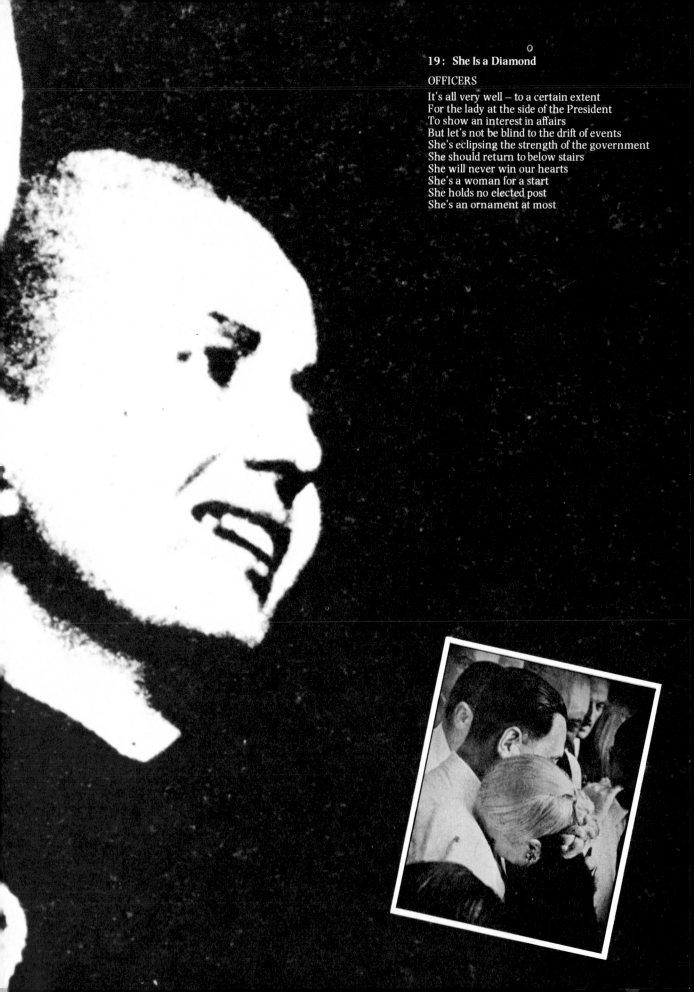

19 : She Is a Diamond

OFFICERS

It's all very well — to a certain extent
For the lady at the side of the President
To show an interest in affairs
But let's not be blind to the drift of events
She's eclipsing the strength of the government
She should return to below stairs
She will never win our hearts
She's a woman for a start
She holds no elected post
She's an ornament at most

There was very little plain sailing for either Peron or Eva in 1951. Their years in charge of the country had been unlike any Argentina had ever seen but beneath the amazing façade of glamour, dynamic action, social justice and public worship of Evita, the nation was falling apart.

The Perons had brought the economy to the verge of ruin; reckless spending on a massive scale had sunk Argentina deep into debt in total contrast to the financial situation they had inherited. Their attempts at redistribution of wealth within Argentina had, as so many such attempts have a habit of doing, resulted in the riches of the few being squandered to no purpose, while the poverty at the other end of the social spectrum remained as widespread as before. The regime had over-industrialized their basically rural country, they had lost millions of pesos when they nationalized operations such as the railways and the telephone which were running smoothly under independent (and usually foreign) control. There is no record of the sums of money that the Perons appropriated for their personal use, but it is reputed to be an enormous sum. Ludicrously generous outbursts of generosity to the odd fortunate could not compensate for the fact that inflation had halved the value of the peso since 1946 — and that the man in the street was now feeling the effects of the financial mismanagement. One of the final blows to his pride must have been the introduction of beef rationing.

The chickens were now coming home to roost and Eva and Peron were losing their following even in areas where their support had hitherto been rock-solid. Eva's personal intervention did nothing to stop a major (and violent) strike of railway workers. The regime adopted murkier methods to enforce their control over dissenting voices and the image of Eva the hatchet woman began to grow up alongside that of Santa Evita. And on top of all this Eva was seriously ill.

PERON

But on the other hand she's all they have
She's a diamond in their dull grey lives, and that's the
Hardest kid of stone — it usually survives
And when you think about it, can you recall
The last time they loved anyone at all?

She's not a bauble you can brush aside
She's been out doing what we just talked about, example:
Gave us back our businesses, got the English out
And if you think about it — well why not do
One or two of the things we promised to?

But on the other hand, she's slowing down
She's lost a little of that magic drive — but I would
Not advise those critics present to derive
Any satisfaction from her fading star
She's the one who's kept us where we are

OFFICERS

She's the one who's kept you where you are

20: Dice Are Rolling/Eva's Sonnet

PERON

Dice are rolling, the knives are out
I see every bad sign in the book
And as far as they can (overweight to a man!)
They have that mean and hungry look

EVA

But we still have the magic we've always had!
The descamisados still worship me
We arrived thanks to them and no one else!
No thanks to your generals – a clutch of stuffed cuckoos!

PERON

It's not a question of a big parade
Proving we're big with the mobs on the street
Our problems are closer than that
They're along the corridor

EVA

You're wrong – the people, my people –

PERON

The people belong to no one!
They are fickle, can be manipulated
Controllable, changeable
In the end the people don't matter – however much they
   love you now
It matters more that as far as my stuffed cuckoos are
   concerned
You don't officially or politically exist!

EVA

So I don't exist!
So I count for nothing!
Try saying that on the street
When all over the world
I am Argentina!
Most of your generals wouldn't even be recognized by
   their own mothers!
But they'll admit I exist when I become vice-president!

PERON

That won't work . . .
We've been through all of this before
They'd fight any attempt to make you vice-president
   tooth and nail
You'd never overcome that sort of opposition with a
   thousand rallies
And even if you did –

EVA

Yes?

PERON

Your little body's slowly breaking down
You're losing speed, you're losing strength – not style.

Eva's solution to their crisis was to announce
that she would run as Vice-Presidential candidate on Peron's ticket at the elections scheduled
for November 1951. (Peron had altered the
constitution making him eligible to run for a
second term of six years.)

It is not clear how this action would have
improved their tottering position in the long run,
but in the short run Eva as a potential Vice
President would doubtless have distracted the
mass of the people from the realities of the country's
situation. They could certainly be persuaded that
the election of their beloved Evita to a government
position for the first time ever would give her the
power she needed to finish her glorious work on
their behalf, which had to date been frustrated by
her lack of official status.

But Eva underestimated the opposition of many
of the generals whose support Peron needed to

That goes on flourishing forever —
But your eyes, your smile
Do not have the sparkle of your fantastic past
If you climb one more mountain it could be your last

EVA

I'm not that ill
Bad moments come but they go
Some days are fine some a little bit harder
But I'm no has-been
It's the same old routine
Have you ever seen
Me defeated?
Don't you forget what I've been through and yet
    I'm still standing —
And if I am ill it could even be to your advantage!

PERON

This is not a case of a sympathetic word in the gossip
    column
Because you've got a cold!
I'm trying to point out that you might die!

This talk of death is chilling, an assault —
Upon ourselves and it will be our fault
If we allow
These morbid septic thoughts
To rule us now
To bring our reason clattering to a halt
I do not need a final sacrifice
Just let me know of any sane device
To shift your strength, your undisputed powers
To places where your mighty deeds
Your golden words
Have not so far cut too much ice

EVA

Then I must now be vice-president!

Those shallow mean pretenders to your throne
Will come to learn ours is the upper hand
For I do not accept this is not known
Already in most quarters of our land
To face the storms so long and not capsize
Is not the chance achievement of a fraud
Conservatives are kings of compromise
So if it suits them, even they'll applaud

And I shall have my people come to choose
Two Perons who shall wear their country's crowns
In thousands in my squares and avenues
Emptying their villages and towns
Where every soul in home or shack or stall
Knows me as Argentina — that is all

Oh I shall be a great vice-president!

*(Instrumental section, during which Eva realises she cannot
    avoid admitting defeat any longer)*

PERON

So what happens now?

(Eva cannot answer. She does not even want to face him)

PERON

So what happens now?

EVA *(in anguish)*

Where am I going to?

PERON

Don't ask any more . . .

(Che bounces in)

govern. She may well have been right about the
loyalty of most of her shirtless ones, but even that
support could not overcome the military's attitude.
No self-respecting general could have contempla-
ted a woman as his Commander-In-Chief which
is what Vice President Eva Peron would become
if Peron died during his second Presidential term.

Ironically, Eva's illness was an even better
guarantee of the continued devotion of her
followers than had she attempted to become
Vice President in full health.

21: Eva's Final Broadcast

CHE

Forgive my intrusion Evita I just had to see
How you admit you have lost! A brand new experience!
 – we
Got it set up!
We fixed you a broadcast
And you're so good on the air!

EVA

The actress hasn't learned the lines you'd like to hear
How could she feel defeated by such cringing
　mediocrities?
She's sad for her country
Sad to be defeated by her own weak body
She's sad for her people
She hopes they will know she did not betray them

(A microphone is switched on. Eva is now on the air)

I want to tell the people of Argentina
I've decided I should decline
All the honours and titles you've pressed me to take
For I'm contented –
Let me simply go on
As the woman who brings her people to the heart of
　Peron!
Don't cry for me Argentina
For the truth is I shall not leave you
Though it may get harder
For you to see me
I'm Argentina
And always will be
Have I said too much? There's nothing more I can think
　of to say to you
But all you have to do is look at me to know that every
　word is true

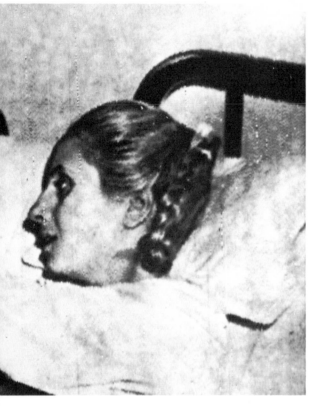

Eva did not abandon her Vice-Presidential ambitions until the very last possible moment. But in the end even she realized that for the first time she would have to admit defeat. Probably her illness forced her to surrender, rather than the army or the fact that demonstrations of public support for Eva were not quite as great as they had been in the past, despite the usual behind-the-scenes Peronist coercion. It is unlikely that the old Eva would have let anything less than death stand in the way of her plans.

Eva made her moving broadcast, turning down the chance of the Vice Presidency that she never really had in the first place, on 31 August 1951.

From that day on her fragile state became Peron's greatest asset as economic, social and political problems crowded around him. On 28 September there was a half-hearted revolt by the army which Peron was able to overcome largely as a result of the incompetence of those rebelling; once again Peron had been saved by the lack of unity within the forces against him.

Eva still tried to continue with her work, but in November she entered hospital and had a four-hour operation. George Pack, an American cancer specialist, took part in the operation, but his participation was kept secret from the patient. The operation was not successful. Eva voted for Peron in the Presidential elections from her hospital bed, the first time women had been allowed to vote in an Argentine election.

The fact that women could vote in this election was one of Eva's genuine achievements; there had never been much pressure from men or women in Argentina's male-dominated society for the extension of the franchise to women, but Eva succeeded in creating a new climate of opinion which encouraged women to seek equality. Female citizens won the right to vote and to run for office in 1947; in 1949 the Peronist Women's Party was set up, with Eva as its President. Peron eventually won a second term of Presidency with an increased share of the vote – he owed a lot to the votes of Argentine women.

The last months of Eva's life were ghastly for her. Her slide into death was slow and painful. Peron made every use of his wife's dramatic condition during his re-election campaign and afterwards until she died. She had had a disruptive effect upon his party as a potential candidate, but as a dying woman she became the perfect focus for public attention, sympathy, admiration and virtual canonization, a distraction from every disaster that the Peronist government had inflicted upon its people. The fact that opposition parties still held meetings was portrayed by Peronists as evil lack of consideration towards a sick woman.

Every possible honour was heaped upon Eva as she faded away. Her last important public pronouncement took place on 17 October 1951, shortly before her operation, delivered from the balcony of the Casa Rosada on the sixth anniversary of her first appearance there. Peron's public tribute to her on this occasion included the statement that she was one of the greatest women humanity had ever known. The day was dedicated to Evita who, on this her final 17 October, made a long and courageous speech urging all who loved her to understand that her life's work had been dedicated to those she loved – her descamisados, her country and Peron. She was superb, and sincere, as convinced as most of her supporters that sainthood was just around the corner. Indeed, Peron announced that 17 October would henceforth be Santa Evita's Day.

In December her book, *La Razon de Ma Vida*, was published, and was of course phenomenally successful. It was a cliché-ridden Peronist tract that revealed little about the author that her speeches had not already given away. Eva was last seen in public on 4 June 1952, the day that Peron was sworn in as President for his second term of six years, which he never completed. She collapsed on that day in the Casa Rosada and never appeared in public again.

22: Montage

In her last hours, images, people and events from her life flow through Eva's mind, while the nation's grief knows no bounds – to the mass of the people she is already a saint, nothing less. Eva hears fragments from:

MAGALDI – 'Eva beware your ambition . . .'

GETTA/WORKERS – 'A new Argentina . . .'

AN OFFICER – 'Statesmanship is more . . .'

FUND MANAGER – 'Accountants only slow things down . . .'

The WALTZ

While choirs sing anthems for the dying, Che breezes in and sings again 'She had her moments . . .'

PERON

High flying, adored, so young, the instant queen, a
Rich beautiful thing of all the talents, a cross between a
Fantasy of the bedroom and a saint
And you were just a backstreet girl
Hustling and fighting
Scratching and biting
High flying, adored, did you believe in your wildest moments
All this would be yours, that you'd become the lady of them all?
Were there stars . . .

Peron having sung Che's song, we now hear Che with some of Peron's words:

CHE

One always picks
The easy fight
One praises fools
One smothers light
One shifts left to right
Practising the art of the possible

(Che has become the Guevara we all know and love)

CHOIR

Santa Santa Evita
Madre de todos los ninos
De los tiranisados
Do los descamisados
De los trabajadores
De la Argentina

On 17 October 1951 ('Loyalty Day') Eva Peron received decorations from the C.G.T., the workers' organization (top left, bottom left and centre). Earlier that year she had received the Great Cross of the Orange Nassau from Prince Bernhard of the Netherlands (top right), and in 1952 (bottom right) she would be granted an award by the Syrian government

CRITICALLY ILL

THE CONDITION OF EVA PERON (ABOVE),
CRITICALLY ILL WIFE OF PRESIDENT JUAN PERON,
HAD DECLINED NOTICEABLY THIS AFTERNOON," THE
ARGENTINE STATE RADIO ANNOUNCED JULY 18. THE
DIAGNOSIS OF MRS. PERON'S ILLNESS HAS NEVER
BEEN OFFICIALLY DISCLOSED. SHE UNDERWENT A
MAJOR OPERATION LAST NOVEMBER AFTER AN EXAMIN-
ATION BY A NEW YORK CANCER AND TUMOR SPECIALIST.

(EDS: THIS IS A FEBRUARY, 1951 FILE PICTURE)

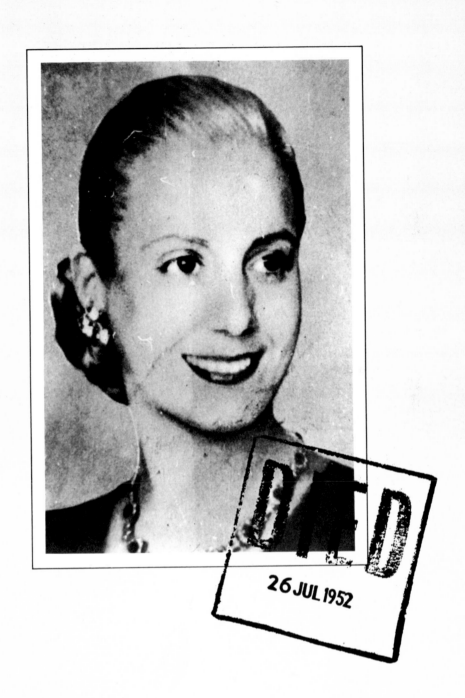

The moment Eva died, on 26 July 1952, with her mother, her sisters and brother and her husband at her side, the embalmers moved in to begin their work of preserving her mortal remains.

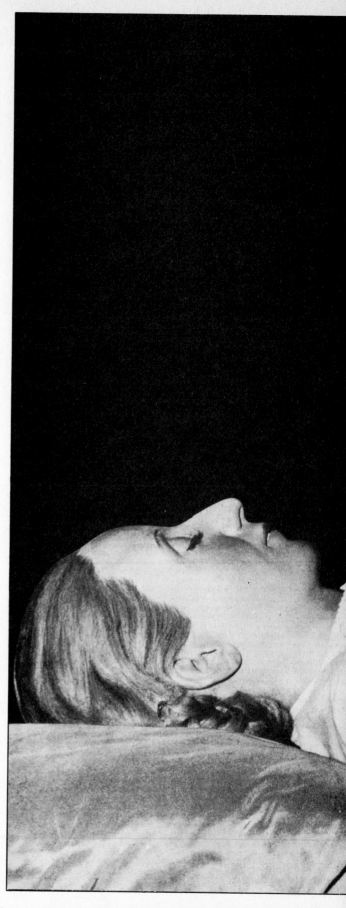

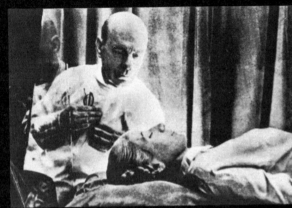

23 : Lament

EVA

The choice was mine and mine completely
I could have any prize that I desired
I could burn with the splendour of the brightest fire
Or else – or else I could choose time

Remember I was very young then
And a year was forever and a day
So what use could fifty, sixty, seventy be?
I saw the lights and I was on my way

And how I lived! How they shone!
But how soon the lights were gone!

The choice was mine and no one else's
I could have the millions at my feet
Give my life to people I might never meet
Or else to children of my own

Remember I was very young then
Thought I needed the numbers on my side
Thought the more that loved me the more loved I'd be
But such things cannot be multiplied

Oh my daughter! Oh my son!
Understand what I have done!

*(The moment Eva dies, embalmers move in to preserve her
fragile body)*

EMBALMERS

Eyes, hair, face, image
All must be preserved
Still life displayed forever
No less than she deserved
Preserved

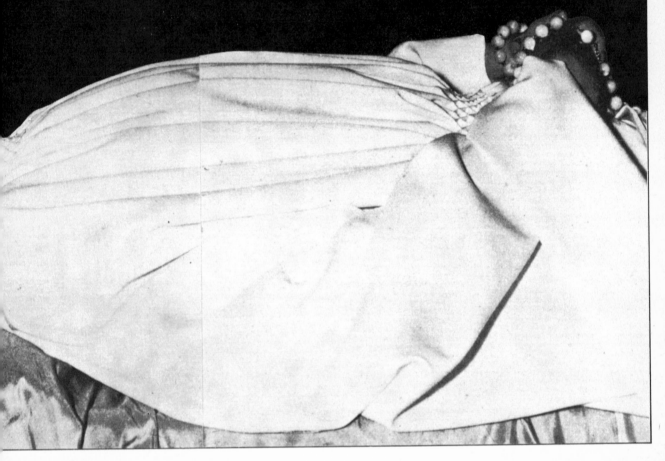

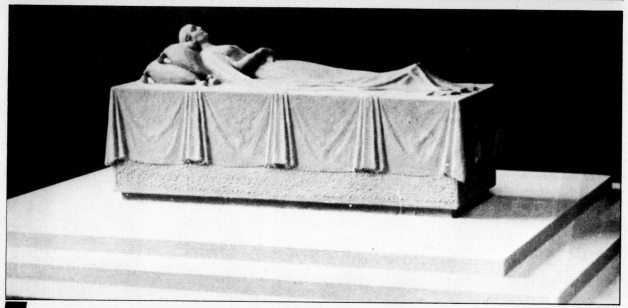

The story of the escapades of the corpse of Eva Peron during the quarter-century after her death is almost as bizarre as the story of her life.

Shortly after Evita died, Peron commissioned the building of what was to be the largest monument in the world in honour of his wife. But the vast architectural enterprise barely got off the drawing board before Peron fell from power, overthrown by the army in 1955. Few Argentinians were sorry to see him go into exile; he had nearly bankrupted the country and even the C.G.T., the guardians of Eva's body, did not support him when the military moved in.

None of the Argentine leaders who followed Peron wanted Eva's final resting place to become a focal point for any kind of political group, which meant that they were unable to bury her anywhere, and they were reluctant to destroy the body. The second of Peron's successors (the first, General Lonardi, lasted a mere four months at the helm), General Aramburu, organized the kidnapping of Eva's body from the C.G.T. headquarters and his secret service smuggled the body out of the country as one of a number of identical coffins. The coffin containing her body eventually wound up in an insignificant grave in the Musocco Cemetery in Milan, under the name of Maria Maggi.

The body of Juan Peron (still alive and well) was also to come to a halt in Europe for many years. He had fled to Paraguay and from there moved on to Panama City. It was there he met an Argentine dancer named Maria Estela Martinez who became his third wife. She was 35 years younger than he was. Peron and Isabelita (as Maria Estela came to be called) moved to Madrid where they lived in grand style. Argentina may have gone broke during Peron's rule, but he certainly had not.

While Peron sat it out in Madrid, Argentina, once the most prosperous and stable state in Latin America, lurched from one catastrophic government to another. From 1955 to 1972 there were eight administrations, none of which halted Argentina's sad slide towards anarchy. Consequently, as those seventeen years went by, more and more people in Argentina (and not just the working class) came to feel that Peron's years in charge were not so bad after all. His decade seemed almost calm and efficient by comparison with the subsequent chaos. Furthermore, it had been blessed with the magic of Evita.

In 1971 Peron finally persuaded Franco to allow him to bring Evita's body to Madrid from its humble grave in Milan. How and when Peron found out about Evita's exact whereabouts will forever remain a mystery, but as Peron's stock slowly improved while he did nothing in Spain one of his ever-increasing number of supporters must have felt that the time was right for Peron to take charge of Argentina's most emotive export, and slipped him the information. It is highly unlikely that no one in Argentina knew where the body was lying, and inevitably one of those in the know, confident that Peron would soon once again be the man to know, made sure that Peron

Models and drawings of the monument to Evita which was never constructed.
Her statue (above left) was to be placed in the central hall,
as noted by the arrow in the drawing above.

was told. Eva's body had survived twenty years remarkably well — her embalmers had done their work well.

Peron and Eva were together again, and as before, it was as a combination that they were at their most powerful. No matter that one half of the team was dead — the legend of Evita had totally recovered from its 1955 setback and in death she held as great a hold on the imaginations of the underprivileged in Argentina as she had in life. Isabelita seemed quite content to accept Evita's body into her home and to become one part of a strange trinity of Perons.

They were of course still in exile in Madrid, but Peron had always maintained contact with fellow countrymen, and these contacts were numerous by 1971. Back in Argentina, Peronistas were surfacing everywhere. The only trouble was that the Peronista party embraced every kind of political opinion. Left-wing, right-wing and centre Peronistas were all convinced that their leader saw their party as representative only of their particular point of view. This was Peron's fault; he had deliberately continued to preach his unworkable doctrine of 'justicialism', allegedly the middle path between capitalism and communism but actually the simultaneous promotion of two mutually exclusive philosophies, in order to appeal to as many potential supporters as possible.

Violence within the ranks of Peron's followers soon became one of the most serious problems the Argentine government had to face. Small wonder then that in 1972, the then President Lanusse became convinced that only the return of the man himself could bring order back to the country. In November 1972, Peron and Isabelita went back to Argentina. Peron was unable to take part in the elections scheduled for March 1973 because he had not been resident in the country for long enough before the election date, but the man elected President, Hector Campora, was a Peron yes-man who campaigned under the slogan 'Campora in Government! Peron in Power!'.

Campora resigned less than two months after his election and in September 1973 Juan Peron was again elected President of Argentina. At last his wife held the post of Vice President, but of course his deputy was not Evita (whose last political ambition had been to hold that office) but Isabelita. At the moment of Peron's final triumph Evita was not by his side, but motionless in Madrid.

But Eva returned in the end to Argentina. On 1 July 1974, only nine months after taking office, Peron died of heart failure brought on by pneumonia. He was in his seventy-ninth year. He had

not had the time to reconcile the warring factions within his own party, let alone tackle any of Argentina's other crises. Isabelita became President, reaching a position of official power which Evita had never come near. But she was no Eva. The two years of her rule were as unhappy as any that poor Argentina had had to endure this century. Before her inevitable fall, Isabelita brought Evita's body back home, but this attempt to strengthen the link between Eva and herself did not save her from the coup that deposed her on 24 March 1976.

PEROИ-PEROИ

Evita's body arrived back in Argentina on 17 November 1974. It remained on display in a crypt at the Presidential residence at Olivos, just outside Buenos Aires, beside the sealed coffin of General Peron. In October 1976, Evita made what must surely be her last journey, to an armoured vault in the Recoleta Cemetery of Buenos Aires. She lies there now, twenty feet underground, watched by guards, protected by the most sophisticated of locks and alarms, and by the strongest of steel walls.

President Videla is now the man struggling to

This 1973 poster invites voters to 'rendez-vous with Peron-Peron'; photos of Peron, Isabelita, and Evita underline the political strength of this strange triumvirate

hold Argentina together. It is a monumental task and he and his government will need some of the qualities of Maria Eva Duarte de Peron if they are to succeed. But not all – it is probably just as well that the crazy, magnificent, demonic complexity that was Evita Peron is no longer inspiring and corrupting the millions from the balcony of the Casa Rosada. If she could, she would; she would not yet be sixty were she alive today.

THE MUSIC OF EVITA

Andrew Lloyd Webber

From the earliest time I can remember I have been interested in musical theatre. What fascinates me most is the way that music can cut corners and say something quite quickly that it would take far longer to say in words. Music can do this by heightening emotions and if the musical structure of the piece is right, it will render unnecessary a lot of explanation. Thus I hope in *Evita* that it doesn't matter that we don't actually see Eva going to Buenos Aires. Although the last line of 'Eva Beware of the City' is Magaldi saying that under no circumstances will he ever take Eva to the big city, somehow music can say that she got her way without it being necessary to explain. I hope it's all there in the key change where the 'Eva Beware of the City' theme is played by the harps and orchestra in C major after Magaldi has sung in A.

Although many opera composers, particularly the romantic ones, were brilliant at cutting corners, lately it has been in the post-war American musical that the technique of really using music as more than the source of a 'hit tune' has blossomed. For me it was Rodgers and Hammerstein who started this ball rolling. There had been attempts before the Second World War to move the musical out of the world of chorus girls or of revue, notably Rodgers and Hart's *Pal Joey* and of course Gershwin who in his opera *Porgy and Bess* anticipated much that I would like to see from contemporary opera by about forty years. But it was *Oklahoma* which first introduced a down-to-earth subject to the musical. It was quite a revelation to kick off with a woman churning butter singing about a beautiful morning. *Oklahoma* really did break all traditions — indeed out of town one critic headlined his review 'No Girls, No Gags, No Chance', although he might have added 'No Tickets' after the New York opening. In my view Rodgers and Hammerstein never really topped *Oklahoma* artistically and started to become sentimental, although there is still obviously much to admire in their work.

Following *Oklahoma*, the Americans produced a whole string of musicals which continually have pushed the frontiers further forward. *Guys and Dolls*, *West Side Story*, and more recently *Cabaret* and *Company* are serious subjects handled in such a way as to suggest that it is in the popular musical theatre that much of the best contemporary theatre music has been composed, and where, significantly, words have equal importance to the music.

But, possibly because I am a composer, I find a snag with the musical. Even in the very finest shows I find worrying that awkward moment when you see the conductor raising his baton and the orchestra lurching into life during the dialogue which indicates the impending approach of music. This is far less annoying in the dance musicals like *A Chorus Line* or *Pippin*, although to my taste the musical underscoring of dialogue is often very sentimental. I have a nagging feeling that the best musicals ultimately give you a sort of exhilarating experience like being in second gear in a fast car: incredibly exciting but hardly very profound. Not that there is anything mere about mere entertainment. It's just that I like to write something where the music and words can get uninterrupted attention without jolts from one style to another. That is why Tim and I chose to write *Evita* with continuous music as we had done with *Jesus Christ Superstar*.

It was Tim's idea to write *Evita*. When he first discussed the idea with me I too was attracted by the subject not solely because of Tim's own enthusiasm. Clearly it provided an extraordinary framework in which to set a big 'aria'. For some time I have worried about a way in which a very obvious melody can be integrated into a hopefully serious dramatic whole without it sounding 'stuck in'. The way to do this with the story of Eva Peron seemed fairly obvious as it was possible to write music for both her public personality and her private one. Eva's public utterances veer between the rabble-rousing extremist (which we have attempted to show in a section such as 'A New Argentina'), to the slightly cynical use of sentimentality ('Don't Cry For Me Argentina'). Thus it was possible to set up a straightforward romantic tune of the kind of 'Don't Cry For Me Argentina' in a dramatic context in which it is valid in its own right, and hopefully does not sound like a big tune stuck in for the sake of a big tune. Immediately she has finished her 'performance' we hear the private side of Eva when she is only interested in how well her speech has gone down with her audience . . . 'Did you hear that? The voice of Argentina,' etc. And afterwards she reverts to her sinister rabble-rousing style when she comes out onto the balcony again to give the workers the bitter as opposed to the sweet side of her public character. Neither Tim nor I really thought that 'Don't Cry For Me Argentina' would be a successful song on its own but we were very gratified to find that it was, because that is where in the opera we tried to show her 'selling' herself to the full.

However when Tim first produced the idea to me, I had certain doubts whether or not there were good reasons for making this an opera in the first place. I felt perhaps it should be a play or maybe a book. It was the possibility of writing about the two sides of Eva's life that most made me feel that music had a dimension to offer, and from then I looked for 'highs' and 'lows' in the story that would work dramatically and musically. It seemed to me that it was crucial to have one romantic theme tune for Eva which would sum up the technique she used to get sympathy.

Thus the melody 'Don't Cry for Me Argentina' was the first thing I wrote for *Evita*, and I composed this ahead of the lyrics.

The second reason for a musical treatment seemed to me the contrast between the sheer vastness of the crowds and the growing isolation of a woman who at the peak of her success found she was dying. The opposition of the military and the aristocracy to the jumped-up actress from the sticks combines effectively with the illness to make a feeling of inevitable doom which I find very exciting to compose for. All of this, I hope, becomes clear in the second half of the second act where musically the opera shifts direction. I think this change, which occurs after her partially successful 'Rainbow Tour' will be more obvious in the theatre as it will combine with her changed visual appearance. It was then she swept her hair back and abandoned her peaches-and-cream hair style of old.

The third and perhaps most decisive reason to make me want to write music for the piece was Tim's idea of the character of Che. He is important because he is Eva's musical alter ego. He is fascinated by her and yet can't stand her. He is jealous and cynical, angry particularly about Peron, but yet despite everything he admires Eva and the argument between them provides not only a device to help explain to the audience some background information, but also leads to the scene which I believe in the theatre could emerge as the core of this side of the opera, the 'Waltz'. Structurally the running argument between Che

and Eva reaches its climax in this obviously 'fantastic' scene. It is a sort of Viennese dream in which these two really rather similarly charismatic characters box and fence and waltz around each other's point of view. I imagine a dance in which they circle around each other but never do they touch. I think that without the character of Che, *Evita* would solely be a sort of musical documentary. Although by its very nature it has to be something of that kind, I hope that, particularly with the guidance of Hal Prince, the revised version which will be staged will add new dimensions and clarify much that was not immediately obvious on record. There was incidentally quite a bit of material that had to be cut from the first recordings because of the length. Our hope is that *Evita* in the theatre will become a specifically theatrical piece that has benefited from the recording studio rather than just being a product of it.

In *Evita* I tried not to self-consciously ape Latin American styles which are obviously not a part of my background. On the record I feel that I maybe bent backwards too far in this respect, and in the theatre I intend to use a more 'Latin' basic rhythm section. However, I am pleased with the use of the harp. Although the harp is found in Argentina only on the Paraguayan border, it seems such an evocative sound of Latin America that it is this that I feel makes the most distinctive contribution to *Evita*'s scoring. Because it is a plucked instrument like the guitar, the definition is tremendous. There is something specifically 'Latin' about the way the chords are spaced by Paraguayan players, normally with a major third sandwiched between the octaves. However, although I am quite pleased with the harp in the *Evita* score, I am glad that I shall have a chance to rework much of the percussion writing in the theatre.

The first recording of *Evita* took five months to make. There were eleven full orchestral sessions with the L.P.O. and as many chorus sessions. A lot of time was spent on the sound. Thus the 'Waltz', which needed a rather brittle translucent quality, was recorded in the very live acoustics of the Henry Wood Hall, whereas 'Don't Cry For Me Argentina' was recorded in the rather ripe woolly acoustics of Studio One at Olympic Sound in Barnes. All the mixing was done at Olympic Sound Studios. After its first performance on tape to an invited audience in July 1976, the whole opera was 're-mixed' and about fifteen minutes of material was cut or re-written.

The 'masters' from which the records were manufactured were 're-cut' about five times; side four which proved specially difficult because of its length was cut nine times in all. Chauvinistically I am glad to say that the pressings all over the world had to come from Britain.

Evita begins with a short introduction in a cinema with a pastiche 1950 film score followed by the spoken announcement of Eva's death. The opera proper starts with the 'Requiem for Evita'. This is the same theme as the closing 'Lament'. Thus the work turns a whole circle musically: if the opera were to continue after the 'Lament', the next sequence would be the 'Requiem'. The sequence in which Che introduces himself and the crowds that is followed by Eva's voice in the first version of 'Don't Cry For Me Argentina' is mirrored, working backwards, in the 'Montage' section and Eva's final broadcast which, I hope, gives the feeling of moving away from Eva's achievements, just as 'Don't Cry For Me Argentina' is the climax of the opening section.

The scene in the café at Junin begins the flashback technique which makes it possible to tell the story. Here again I hope that by the use of a pastiche of a bad night-club song following hard on the climax of the funeral section it is musically clear what has happened without too much explanation. The first line that Eva sings, 'To think that a man / As famous as you are / Could love a poor little nothing like me', is the motif that is used to show Eva on the move. It is used as the opening section in the scene where Eva turns Peron's mistress out of Peron's flat. It is used to show Eva's excitement backstage after 'Don't Cry For Me Argentina'. Eventually it becomes more bitter or sad such as in the 'Rainbow Tour' section or the orchestral introduction of 'High Flying Adored'. But the last word on the theme goes to Che who twists it onto Eva before the Final Broadcast. This short theme is musically to the private character of Eva what 'Don't Cry For Me Argentina' is to the public. Eva has another important theme which is not a song as such. This first appears in the middle section ('Bad is good for me, I'm bored . . .' etc.) of 'Eva Beware of the City'. It is used to show her demanding to get her way (the beginning of 'Rainbow High') or coaxing to get it as at the end of the 'New Argentina' section where she turns the charm on Peron. It is also placed at the end of that scene to show a slight, if intended, vulnerability on Eva's part. It softens her after the hardness of 'A New Argentina' so as to, hopefully, win her a few hearts for her entrance on the balcony of the Casa Rosada.

There are two other themes that are important to the structure of the 'private' characterization of Eva. One appears in the opera first in the song 'Goodnight and Thank You' in the passage 'There is no one, no one at all, never has been'. I decided that it was best to set this very cynical lyric with an orchestration a bit like a drunken brass band. First it appears sung by Eva and Che, then by Peron — indeed the announcer introduces Peron with a short section of it before the Casa Rosada scene. But it reaches its conclusion in the 'Waltz' where Eva used it to answer Che back.

The other 'plot' theme first appears in the harp solo after Peron and Eva have sung their version of 'There is no one'. I refer to this as the death theme. It is the one that combines with the 'It must be a dream' motif to kill Eva. Thus it recurs often in the second half of the second act — in the long argument between Eva and Peron and finally sung by Che ('Forgive my intrusion Evita, I just have to see . . .'). The harp solo in the first act is supposed to give the first inkling of Eva's doomed career. She has just met Peron, indeed the solo could represent her sleeping with him for the first time, but it combines with the death theme at the end with the bass line of the middle section of 'I'd Be Surprisingly Good For You'. I have tried to reserve this line for sections where the idea of inevitable forces gathering momentum is required. Eva has it first. Peron has it next. The bass line is to the fore when Peron speaks of dice that are rolling and knives that are out towards the end of each act. Thus I hope the allusion to these two themes in the harp solo sets Eva's triumphant scenes in a frame which we know is ultimately doomed.

I hope that I have made clear by all this where my sympathies lie. I find Eva Peron a very unsympathetic character, easily the most unpleasant character about whom I have written — except perhaps Peron himself. Yet I find her story fascinating, perhaps because there are lessons to be learned from the objectionable way in which the Perons manipulated people and their prejudices that is not so far removed from certain activities in contemporary Britain. And yet, perhaps because she died when she did, it is hard not to admire something about her. She must have been furious when she found that she was ill. That is why her story intrigues me. I am sure that Puccini would have adored her.

Andrew Lloyd Webber was born in 1948, the elder son of W. S. Lloyd Webber, principal of The London College of Music. He was a Queens Scholar at Westminster School and then, after one term at Magdalen College, Oxford, went to study music at the Guildhall School of Music and the Royal College of Music. His first music to be published was a piano suite written when he was nine. He composed the score to Alan Ayckbourn's book and lyrics for *Jeeves*, the film scores for *Gumshoe* and *The Odessa File*, and has recently released a series of variations on the Paganini theme. He is married, with one daughter.

Tim Rice, born in 1944, attended Lancing College, Sussex, and then the Sorbonne. After studying law

he spent three years in the record industry. A regular radio and television broadcaster, he is also co-compiler of *The Guinness Book of British Hit Singles*, and has edited the *Heartaches Cricketers' Almanack* since 1975. He is married, and has two children.

Andrew Lloyd Webber, composer, and Tim Rice, lyricist, met in 1965. Their first success came in 1968 with the pop oratorio *Joseph and the Amazing Technicolor Dreamcoat*, which is still performed in schools and in the professional theatre throughout the world The rock opera *Jesus Christ Superstar* followed in 1970, and has since been staged in sixteen countries, and filmed, in 1973, by Norman Jewison. *Evita* is their most recent work.

BIBLIOGRAPHY

Barager, Joseph R., ed. *Why Peron Came To Power* (Borzoi, New York, 1968) Twenty-two separate articles, including a short extract from Eva's book *La Razon de mi Vida*.

Bourne, Richard. *Political Leaders Of Latin America* (Pelican, London, 1969) Six excellent essays on six notable Latin Americans, including pieces on both Eva Peron and Che Guevara.

Cowles, Fleur. *Bloody Precedent* (Random House, New York, 1952) Written before Eva's death. Perons compared to Juan and Encarnacion Rosas, Argentine dictators of the nineteenth century.

Harbinson, W. A. *Evita, A Legend For The Seventies* (Star Books, London, 1977) Eva given the Elvis Monthly treatment.

Main, Mary. *The Woman With The Whip* (Corgi, London, 1977) Written in 1952, after Eva's death, but not published in Britain until 1977. Short epilogue added for 1977 edition outlining the story of Peron and of Eva's body since her death. A superb biography.

Owen, Frank. *Peron: His Rise and Fall* (Cresset Press, London, 1957) The story of Peron until his fall from power in 1955; naturally includes the story of Eva.

Acknowledgements
The majority of photographs in this book were supplied by the authors. The publishers gratefully acknowledge the following for permission to reproduce copyright photographs: Associated Press; Camera Press; Colorific Photo Library Ltd (photos © Time, Inc; by Thomas McAvoy and Michael Rougier); Editorial Sudamericana; Keystone Press; Douglas McCreath; Popperfoto; Rex Features; Siete Oias Illustrados; Star Books; Thames Television; John Topham Picture Library. Every effort has been made to trace the copyright holders of the photographs used in this volume. Should there be any omissions in this respect, we apologise and shall be pleased to make the appropriate acknowledgement in future editions.